⋇

The Power of Humility

Fr. Canice Bourke, O.F.M. Cap.

The Power of Humility

Why Humility Must Be
the Heart of Your Spiritual Life —
and How to Make It So

SOPHIA INSTITUTE PRESS®
Manchester, New Hampshire

The Power of Humility was originally published as *Humility: The Foundation of the Spiritual Life* (Westminster, Maryland: The Newman Press, 1951). This 2002 edition by Sophia Institute Press contains revisions to the original text, including minor editorial revisions to eliminate ambiguities, the addition of subheadings, the omission of the preface, and the division of the original Chapter Four into two chapters.

Cover design by Lorraine Bilodeau

On the cover: Single Dandelion Seed © Derek P. Redfearn/Getty Images/The Image Bank

Sophia Institute Press®
Box 5284, Manchester, NH 03108
1-800-888-9344
www.sophiainstitute.com

Nihil obstat: Jacobus P. Bastible, *Censor Deputatus*
Imprimatur: Daniel, *Espiscopus Corcagiensis*
October 17, 1950
Imprimatur: Fr. Colmanus Doneraile, Min. Prov.
October 19, 1950

Library of Congress Cataloging-in-Publication Data

Canice, Father, O.F.M. Cap., b. 1890.
    The power of humility : why humility must be the heart of
    your spiritual life — and how to make it so / Canice Bourke. —
    [Rev. ed.].
    p. cm.
    Rev. ed. of: Humility. 1951.
    Includes bibliographical references.
    ISBN 1-928832-45-8 (pbk. : alk. paper)
    1. Humility. 2. Spiritual life — Catholic Church. I. Canice,
    Father, O.F.M. Cap., b. 1890. Humility. II. Title.
    BV4647.H8 C3 2002
    241'.4 — dc21   2002000293

02 03 04 05 06 07 08 10 9 8 7 6 5 4 3 2 1

For Mary

Contents

Editor's note: The biblical quotations in the following pages are taken from the Douay-Rheims edition of the Old and New Testaments. Where applicable, quotations have been cross-referenced with the differing names and enumeration in the Revised Standard Version, using the following symbol: (RSV =).

⚜

The Power of Humility

Chapter One

Heaven is for the humble

There was the noise of sandaled footsteps on the road; voices were heard — loud, argumentative, insistent. It was the Apostles walking to Capharnaum. They were disputing on the journey. Our blessed Lord wended His way rather apart from them, communing with His eternal Father. Now and again the sound of the strife in words reached His ears.

When they had arrived at the town and had gotten to the house to which they were traveling, our Lord turned around and inquired what subject they had been discussing. An awkward silence fell over them; no one answered, for they would have felt a sense of shame in admitting that the question argued was which of them would be the greatest man. After a while they ventured to refer it to our Lord, and they asked Him for His opinion: "Who, thinkest Thou, is the greater in the kingdom of Heaven?"[1] This afforded an occasion for the gentle Son of God to give us one of His most vital messages.

Carefully He prepared the setting of it to impress it the more deeply. He vested His words in external circumstances, the surer to fix them in their minds. In the house there happened to be a child who perhaps belonged to the family who dwelled there. He was probably about five years of age. Our Lord beckoned to him. With a shy hesitancy, he approached. Around him Christ put His divine arms encouragingly and placed him in the midst of the Apostles. There the little boy stood, simply and artlessly, while the men about him waited for the answer to their query.

At last our Lord spoke: "Amen, I say to you, unless you be converted and become as little children, you shall not enter into the kingdom of Heaven." This was not a direct answer, but it was a very definite instruction. Then immediately they heard the full reply to the question they had posed. "Whosoever, therefore, shall

[1]   Matt. 18:1.

humble himself as this little child, he is the greater in the kingdom of Heaven."[2] They knew at once, as they reflected on the Master's teaching, that a change must be made in themselves: "unless you be converted" — from being proud they must change to being humble. This was the indispensable condition for entrance into the kingdom. And they understood that it was also the essential thing for greatness in the kingdom.

ↄ⋆

*Christ continually reveals
the need for humility*

Those divine words are meant for a far more numerous audience than the group of Apostles in the house at Capharnaum that day. They are addressed to every Christian who wants to secure salvation.

We must not fail to notice the emphasis with which our Lord spoke when He uttered them. He said, "Amen, I say to you." That phrase calls for special attention to the fact that no man can achieve his supernatural destiny without being humble — that no human being can entertain any hope of the happiness of Heaven without

[2] Matt. 18:3-4.

the presence, in some degree, of the virtue of humility in his soul.

The Gospel tells us of other instances when our Lord enjoined this virtue upon us. Actually three of His parables were composed for the express purpose of inculcating it. There was the famous description of the Pharisee and the publican praying in the Temple. Our Lord pictures the two men as the personification of pride and humility respectively; He shows us the violent contrast in their prayers. So effectively does it strike our mind that we recoil from the fatuous glorying of the one, and we are drawn to the humbleness of the other. He finishes the story with the words: "Everyone that exalteth himself shall be humbled; and he that humbleth himself shall be exalted."[3]

There was the parable of the last place at the feast. It was told on an occasion when He had observed men who were filled with an idea of their self-importance selecting prominent positions for themselves at table. "When thou art invited," He said, "go, sit down in the lowest place: that when he who invited thee cometh, he may say to thee: Friend, go up higher." And again our

---

[3] Luke 18:14.

Lord finishes with the words "Everyone that exalteth himself shall be humbled; and he that humbleth himself shall be exalted."[4] He repeats them for the third time when he warns the people not to imitate the Scribes and Pharisees in their love for the first chairs in the synagogues.[5] This threefold repetition has a significance that should be noted.

The last of the parables on humility describes a man coming from the farm at evening and being told by his employer to prepare the supper and to sit down to eat only after the employer himself has taken his meal. The worker is not thanked for doing the labor he was contracted to do.

Then comes the message from our Lord: "So you also, when you shall have done all these things that are commanded you, say: We are unprofitable servants; we have done that which we ought to do."[6] Those divine words are unmistakable. If, by God's grace, we are keeping our feet on the narrow path, if we are doing all those things that are commanded, still there must be

[4] Luke 14:10-11.
[5] Matt. 23:12.
[6] Luke 17:10.

humility in us; still we must esteem ourselves as useless servants.

We know not the relative numbers of saved and lost. That vast and final question is entirely hidden. Solely to the Godhead is known the number of the elect who are to be placed in supernal beatitude. Our divine Lord was asked, "Are there few saved?" All He said in reply was, "Strive to enter by the narrow gate; for many, I say to you, shall seek to enter and shall not be able."[7] He did not lift the veil that hangs over this tremendous vision of the future. But whoever is in Hell is a proud man, for there a humble man could not go. There never was and never shall be a humble man banished from God.

In imagination we picture the Last Judgment of mankind when the sign of the Cross will appear in the skies over the heads of the millions of assembled men. On the clouds Christ the Judge will come in power and majesty. The human race will be divided into two groups on that great day of the Lord.

He tells us Himself that He "will save the humble of spirit."[8] They will be placed on His right hand.

---

[7] Luke 13:23-24.
[8] Ps. 33:19 (RSV = Ps. 34:18).

He warns us that "he that holdeth pride shall be filled with maledictions, and it shall ruin him in the end,"[9] and that "every proud man is an abomination to Him."[10] Moreover, we have it on the authority of the leading theologian in the Church that by pride, more than by any other vice, man is turned away from God. Ranged on the left hand of the Judge are the proud, and in ultimate ruin they depart. . . .

As we proceed with our study of the virtue of humility, it will become clear to us why our blessed Lord has solemnly warned us that unless we become converted from our pride and become like children in their humility, we shall never set foot in His kingdom above.

---

[9] Ecclus. 10:15 (RSV = Sir. 10:13).
[10] Prov. 16:5.

Chapter Two

⚜

What humility is

What exactly is humility? Of the various Christian virtues, it is probable that humility has the misfortune of being the least understood. Indeed, we are told that it is only the person who has acquired it who really grasps the nature of it. St. Lawrence Justinian[11] remarks that no one can well understand what humility is unless God gives him the gift of being humble; for there is nothing in which men are more often mistaken than in their notions of what constitutes humility.

This much must be said at the outset: the bare speculative study of this virtue avails little in its acquisition.

---

[11] St. Lawrence Justinian (1381-1455), first Patriarch of Venice.

The Power of Humility

Our reading and investigation must be accompanied by many a prayer that God in His mercy may grant it to us. If He did not condescend to do so, in vain would we apply our mind to the consideration of the subject.

St. Francis de Sales[12] sees a danger in even praising humility. On account of hearing such eulogies of it, we might begin to practice the virtue through self-love. This, of course, would be a very faulty approach and one destined to end in failure.

⚜

Humility demands that you
recognize your own nothingness

If humility is the least understood of virtues, it is also the most variously defined. From the different definitions given by authors, a few will now be selected. They have the advantage of clarifying parts or aspects of the virtue.

St. Thomas Aquinas states that humility is the virtue that restrains our will from tending immoderately toward great things.[13] He explains that it is proper to

---

[12] St. Francis de Sales (1567-1622), Bishop of Geneva.

[13] St. Thomas Aquinas (1225-1274; Dominican philosopher, theologian, and Doctor), *Summa Theologica*, II-II, Q. 161, art. 1.

this virtue for a man to repress in himself the desire of things that are above him, and that in its essence it means a certain praiseworthy depreciation or lowering of ourselves to the last degree.

St. Bernard and St. Bonaventure say that humility is a virtue by which a man, through a true knowledge of himself, becomes worthless in his own eyes.[14]

Some theologians define humility as a supernatural virtue that inclines a man, out of reverence for God, to abase himself and hold himself in the place he knows is his due. Others regard it as the virtue that makes us recognize our complete dependence on God, our powerlessness and our nothingness, and which prevents us from despising others or from raising ourselves above them.

In the careful reading of these definitions, certain words hold our attention; the mind singles out some notes and retains them: *knowledge of self, reverence for God, self-depreciation, our nothingness, complete dependence on God.* All these things are elements composing the virtue.

[14] St. Bernard (1090-1153), abbot of Clarivaux; St. Bonaventure (c. 1217-1274; Franciscan theologian, known as the Seraphic Doctor), *Quaest. disp. de Perf. Evang.*, I.

The Power of Humility

⁂

To be humble, you must know yourself

To acquire humility, self-knowledge is absolutely essential. No man can be humble if he does not know himself thoroughly.

The saints understood the grave need of this knowledge. Some of their prayers are familiar. St. Augustine[15] used to say, "Lord, may I know myself and may I know Thee." St. Francis of Assisi[16] would exclaim, "Who art Thou, Lord, and what am I?"

To know ourselves is one of the most precious graces that God can bestow. We should implore it frequently of Him.

If we fail in self-knowledge, we shall fail in our knowledge of Him, for the two knowledges are closely connected. One leads to the other. It is not possible to come to an adequate knowledge of God except by a true knowledge of self. And nobody rightly knows himself if he does not bear in mind his own nothingness.[17] "If any

---

[15] St. Augustine (354-430), Bishop of Hippo.

[16] St. Francis of Assisi (1182-1226), founder of the Franciscan Order.

[17] *Quaest. disp. de Perf. Evang.*, I.

man think himself to be something, whereas he is nothing, he deceiveth himself."[18]

To assist us in our fact-finding about self, St. Bonaventure says that all our sins are due to negligence or passion or malice. When we realize that our offenses originate in one or another of these causes, we begin to understand ourselves. And unless, in our recollection of our past sins, we put our finger on the precise cause of each sin, we shall never reach the goal of perfect self-knowledge.[19]

When we know ourselves as we really are in God's sight, the vain and unreasonable opinion we have of self immediately vanishes. We see how very vain and very unreasonable such vanity is because we discover within ourselves only nothingness and sin. This is humble-mindedness. It is important. It is a necessary condition of humility. It is the ground we have for being humble.

But it is not humility; it is only knowledge. And no virtue exists in knowledge merely. Not in the intellect is virtue found; rather it is always in the will. At a later

[18] Gal. 6:3.

[19] St. Bonaventure, *Holiness of Life*, trans. Laurence Costello (St. Louis: B. Herder, 1928), 2.

stage we shall consider the fact of our nothingness. But meanwhile it must be noted that the knowledge of this fact does not make us humble. This mere theoretical knowledge is easily attained, but by itself it is useless.

There is knowing and knowing. We know, for instance, that we shall certainly die. We shall know it in a different way when the doctor says we have but a few weeks to live. We shall then *realize* the knowledge. We know, too, that God is everywhere, but how few there are who realize it. In the same way, we may know of our nothingness. But only by God's grace do we fully realize it and become intimately conscious of it. It is no longer speculative. It is practical. And it must be accompanied by a proper sense of our sinfulness. This is what the masters mean by true self-knowledge.

※

*Humble-mindedness leads you
to subject yourself to God*

On true self-knowledge, as on an essential basis, humility is founded. Humble-mindedness leads us on to humble-heartedness; that is, it gives rise by a natural consequence to humility in the heart or will. When we have attained, by the help of God, to a true knowledge of self, we come to entertain a disesteem and even a contempt for self.

True self-knowledge means that we do not think ourselves to be above what we are or more than we are.[20] This makes our will act. Our will holds in check our urge to tend immoderately to great things, to exalt ourselves above our deserts. From the light God has given us on self we come to depreciate self. And out of this self-abasement there follows a due subjection to God. In this subjection we have the essence of the virtue. Humility principally consists in the subjection of man to God.[21] This subordination must exist in us at least to the extent of avoiding grave sin.

Pride, on the contrary, gets rid of the sense of subjection to God. We see it in the parable of the prodigal son.[22] He wanted to be free of the restraint in his father's house; he wished to get away from subjection.

Self-contempt should not be regarded as an extravagant notion or as something reserved for the use of saints. Indeed, it is regarded by theologians as the first act or

[20] *Summa Theologica*, II-II, Q. 161, art. 6.

[21] Ibid., art. 2.

[22] Luke 15:11-32.

function of humility.[23] Our Lord Himself bids us call ourselves "unprofitable servants."[24] *Unprofitable* means useless. What is useless or of no account is held in contempt. St. Bonaventure assures us that the act of the virtue is holding ourselves to be of no account.[25] If we honestly consider our past offenses, we shall come to entertain that opinion. It could perhaps be said that when we ponder on our *nothingness*, we are led to a *disesteem* for self, and when we reflect on our *sins*, we are led to a *contempt* for self.

Nor may we consider this idea of the nothingness of man as an unjustifiable term or as an exaggeration. The expression is quite true. It is God's word. We have already seen that God, through St. Paul, tells us that a man is guilty of self-deception if he thinks himself to be something, "whereas he is nothing."

"Love to be unknown and accounted as naught," counsels the *Imitation of Christ*.[26] No easy matter is it to

---

[23] Billuart, *Cursus Theol.*, 205.

[24] Luke 17:10.

[25] *Quaest. disp. de Perf. Evang.*, I.

[26] Thomas à Kempis, *Imitation of Christ*, Bk. 1, ch. 2, no. 3.

follow this advice, for the reason that we are not sufficiently grounded in the knowledge and contempt of self. Our self-love prevents us from sincerely making our own those words of Job: "I have sinned, and indeed I have offended, and I have not received what I have deserved."[27] We might say them of ourselves, but if others used them about us, we would resent it; we could not take the insult because there is no genuine interior humility in us. We do not apply the words to ourselves in the spirit of truth.

◆

Reverence and truth are essential to humility

There is one element in the virtue that must be well marked: reverence for God. It is a primary and essential thing. If it be lacking, humility cannot exist. Reverence for God is the very source and origin of it. St. Thomas states, "Humility is caused by divine reverence." And quite definitely again, "Of humility in the mind as well as of humility in the heart, the principle and root is the reverence which a person has for God."[28]

[27] Job 33:27.
[28] *Summa Theologica*, II-II, Q. 161, arts. 4-6.

The Power of Humility

When a mortal is confronted by the Lord or when he kneels before the tabernacle and dwells prayerfully on the divine perfections — the holiness, the power, the immensity of God — he sees the overwhelming contrast between God and himself. He recognizes his absolute inferiority before these infinite attributes. He acknowledges his entire dependence on God. He adores; and in this act of supreme worship, the enormous antithesis is apparent to him: his own lowliness and nothingness is contrasted with the immeasurable greatness and immense majesty of the Lord. When, in the act of homage, he regards God, he adores Him; when he regards himself, he lowers and depreciates himself. It is precisely at that moment of self-abasement, that instant of self-annihilation, that the virtue of humility is born in him. From a revering of the Godhead it takes its rise.[29]

Humility, one must never forget, is founded on the truth. It really is a matter of truth. It observes the rule of right reason according to which a person has a true opinion of himself.[30] This true opinion is the knowledge

---

[29] Cf. Columba Marmion, *Christ, the Ideal of the Monk*, ch. 11.

[30] *Summa Theologica*, II-II, Q. 162, art. 3.

of our inherent nothingness. When the humble man looks upon himself in relation to God, he can in all truthfulness choose the lowest place, as our Lord told those who were invited to the feast to do. In comparison with the Almighty, his self-depreciation can go down to the very last degree. He always remembers our blessed Savior's statement: "Without me you can do nothing,"[31] and he recognizes well the fact that of himself he is nothing and can do nothing. But he also remembers what St. Paul said: "I can do all things in him who strengtheneth me."[32] He realizes that by the divine assistance, he can do things that, if left to his own resources, he never could accomplish.

✢

Humility demands moderation
in self-esteem and in desire for esteem

In human nature, there is a tendency toward self-esteem. It is a lawful and useful tendency: a man must esteem himself if he desires to live properly. But it is a tendency that has to be watched, because if carried too

[31] John 15:5.
[32] Phil. 4:13.

far, it develops into pride. There must be self-esteem, but there must also be self-contempt. The contradiction is only a seeming one. It is quite clear that a man cannot do both things, esteem himself and despise himself, from the same standpoint. They have to be done from different angles. St. Bonaventure explains the difficulty by saying that "by reason of his being *deiform*, man must be honored because there shines in him a divine image and likeness; by reason of his being *defectible*, he can be esteemed of little value; and by reason of his *deformity* [that is, through sin], he can be judged of no account — not to insult him, but for the honor of God, who has been outraged by sin."[33] So, then, under the aspect of his being made to the image and likeness of God, a man should duly esteem himself; and under the aspect of his being sinful and prone to sin, he must despise himself.

There is also in us a tendency to gain the esteem of others. It is necessary to have people's esteem if we are to live in their society. Our honor and our personal dignity are involved in this tendency. But it is one that, like our self-esteem, must be well supervised, because the immoderate desire for the esteem of others is vanity.

[33] *Quaest. disp. de Perf. Evang.*, I.

It snarls the conduct of our life. Instead of having God as the final purpose of our actions, we work for the honor of success and the distinction of praise. This is a violation of the rights of the Lord.

✻

Consider the violet as an image of humility

St. Bonaventure amplifies his definition of humility in characteristic Franciscan fashion. He sees an image of the virtue in the violet. Apparently the idea of the modest violet goes back for centuries.

"The size," he says, "the position, the perfume, and the color of this flower all show that it is an emblem of humility. Its size is very small — what flower indeed is less? The humble are small in their own eyes. The apostle who had labored more than the rest says, 'I am the least of the apostles, who am not worthy to be called an apostle.' The position of this flower is quite close to the earth, and you have St. Paul's exhortation not to mind high things, but to consent to the humble. Those who think themselves better than others or who wish to appear better than others do not share this quality of the flower. . . . They who are small in their own estimation have the size of the violet; but if they wish to be raised above others exteriorly, they have not the position of the violet. . . . The perfume is pleasant and healthy. Even the proud praise humility: by the praiseworthiness is understood the pleasure of the perfume. It is health-giving also, for it sometimes happens that those who hear the praises of the virtue become better themselves. The color is subdued, but to one who knows the flower, this but makes it commendable and delightful."[34]

⚜

Subject yourself to others,
mindful of God's presence in them

We now proceed to consider the virtue in another way. Not only must we be humble before God, but we must be humble before our fellow creatures as well. And strange as it may at first appear, this virtue operates in much the same fashion when we are in the presence of our fellowman as when we are in the presence of God.

Consider for a moment the question of obedience. We carry out the instructions of those over us because the authority they have is divine. It is God whom we obey in them. Similarly, with regard to fraternal charity,

[34] *Tract. de Vit. Myst.*, ch. 17, no. 53.

we love all human creatures because they are manifestations of God, because divine goodness is shown in them. It is God whom we love in them. And it is for the identical reason that we humble ourselves before them: it is to God in them that we humble ourselves. Divine reverence makes us lower ourselves before God; it makes us lower ourselves before what is of God in every living man. St. Thomas's words are "We ought to revere God not only in Himself, but we ought also to revere what is of Him in all persons; but not with the same degree of reverence that we give to God."[35]

The famous Pauline phrase is that we must be obedient to men, not as to men, but as to the Lord.[36] In the presence of a superior we see one thing, the man, but we obey another thing, the Lord's authority in him. It is the same with humility. We subject ourselves to men, not as to men, but as to the Lord. In the presence of a human being, we see one thing and we humble ourselves to another thing. We see the man of flesh and blood, and we subject ourselves to him as a child of God. We take ourselves in one capacity — naturally; but we take him in

[35] *Summa Theologica*, II-II, Q. 161, art. 3.
[36] Cf. Eph. 6:7.

another capacity — supernaturally. We rightly deem our natural self to be beneath him regarded supernaturally — that is, as a son of God, as a brother of Christ, as a temple of the Holy Spirit, or as a child of the Blessed Mother.

St. Thomas makes a distinction that is very useful. Two things, he explains, may be considered in man: what the man is of himself and what there is of God in him. Whatever points to fault is of the man himself; whatever makes for salvation or perfection is of God.[37]

Now, it is a principle that what is inferior be subject to what is superior, and that what is defective be subject to what is perfect: that is, man to God, nature to grace, the natural to the supernatural. In that subjection lies, as we have seen, the essence of humility. And the law of the virtue, therefore, requires that we submit our nature to the gifts of God with reverence, whether those gifts be in ourselves or in others. Every man ought to subject what is of his own nature to the more excellent things that come from God, wherever they may be.[38]

---

[37] *Summa Theologica*, II-II, Q. 161, art. 3.

[38] William Ullathorne, *Groundwork of Christian Virtue*, 133.

⚜

Esteem others as better than you

That is how the virtue is exercised toward our fellows. It is a reverence given, not to human nature, but to the gifts of God in that nature. We bow down our nature, in a sense of our inferiority, to what has come from God. This spirit of humility is often seen in a truly Catholic people; it is shown in a general habit of mutual respect, in reverence, in gentleness, in courtesy. It is born of grace, although a person without faith might consider it only an unusual politeness.[39]

St. Paul's advice to the Philippians was this: "In humility let each esteem others better than himself,"[40] and St. Peter counseled, "Be ye subject to every human creature for God's sake."[41] St. Thomas considers the question of this counsel, whether a man ought to subject himself through humility to all.[42] We have his assurance that there is no danger of falsity, no room for error, if we esteem ourselves beneath everybody in the world. It is

[39] Ibid.
[40] Cf. Phil. 2:3.
[41] 1 Pet. 2:13.
[42] *Summa Theologica,* II-II, Q. 161, art. 3.

therefore possible to fulfill the two apostles' exhortations without any insincerity. How St. Thomas explains it is that a man can esteem some good in his fellowman that he himself does not possess; hence, he can subject himself to that person through humility. And a man can acknowledge some evil in himself that is not in his neighbor, and from this consideration again he can put himself beneath that person.

Observe that it is not required for humility that we deem the gifts of God to us to be inferior to what appear to be the gifts of God in another. We may prefer our own.[43] But, of course, if we received greater gifts, we should be all the more humble, especially if we have not corresponded with these favors. Neither is it necessary that we consider our own sins to be worse than the sins of our neighbor; otherwise each person would look upon himself as a greater sinner than anybody else.[44]

At the same time, we can sincerely and truthfully esteem others better than ourselves and subject ourselves to them for God's sake. The Franciscan Doctor St. Bonaventure shows us how. When a person suffers from

[43] Ibid.
[44] Ibid.

some serious complaint, this ailment is naturally far more real to him than the greatest sufferings of other men. He feels it much more than he feels the anguish of others. And even though the sufferings of others may be very great, to him his sufferings are the greatest. Every man is miserable; he is aware of that; but his own personal misery comes home to him the most keenly of all.

In the same way, the person who realizes his own sins and faults feels them more deeply than he can feel the sins and faults of any other individual. They are much more real to him. He knows well the many reasons he has for being true to God, and he is therefore all the more conscious of his own ingratitude. He knows himself better than he knows anybody; he feels the guilt of his own sins more intimately than he feels the offenses of other people. From this deeper sense and fuller knowledge, he judges that his own sins are greater than theirs and that he himself is less worthy than they. "For this reason," adds the saint, "a man must deem himself below others, *not because he is certain that he is*, but because he is *more certain of his own worthlessness* than he is of theirs."[45]

---

[45] *Quaest. disp. de Perf. Evang.*, I.

The Power of Humility

We know in one way that there are coins in the bank, but we know in quite another way that there are coins in our own pocket. We arrive, then, at the conclusion that it is reasonable to place ourselves beneath men who are in every way our inferiors and that it is truthful to act as though we were inferior to all. When we do so, we can regard what we have of ourselves, which is nothingness and sin, in comparison with what others have of God, which is much. And even on the supposition that there is some gift in us that is quite obvious and that appears to give us superiority over a person, still without any pretense we may truly consider that there can be something hidden in him, some unseen good quality by which he is superior to us. Both St. Thomas and St. Bonaventure quote this principle.[46] When, therefore, we subject ourselves to an equal or to an inferior, when we place ourselves beneath him, it is because we take him to be our superior in some respect. Of every man we can sincerely say what the Baptist said of our Lord: "He is before me."[47]

---

[46] *Summa Theologica*, II-II, Q. 161, art. 3; *Quaest. disp. de Perf. Evang.*, I.

[47] Cf. John 1:27.

Persons in authority should seldom *show* this subjection, but they may and should have it internally. To manifest it exteriorly might run counter to another principle: the dignity of their position must be upheld.

To sum up, then, and set forth the doctrine clearly once more: it is unquestionable that all men are not equal in merit, that one is better than another and that one person is superior to his fellows. Humility never departs from the truth; it acts by making each of us consider what he has *of himself* — his nothingness and his sins — and it makes us consider in our neighbor what he has *from God* — his virtues, his gifts of nature and of grace. At the contrast, we should acknowledge our inferiority and humble ourselves. Furthermore, each one, without any error, can believe himself to be beneath everybody on account of his own secret sins of which he is conscious and on account of the gifts of that are hidden from his eyes in others.[48]

Few there are, however, who get as far as this in the virtue. Their self-knowledge does not go deep enough. It is a grace not given to all. A special light from the Holy Spirit is needed so that they can gaze intensely at

[48] *Summa Theologica*, II-II, Q. 161, art. 5.

the divine perfections and also see down into their own selves and then, beholding their native nothingness in the presence of the greatness of God, and considering His gifts in others, place themselves at the feet of all.[49]

⚜

Practice the actions that
help you develop humility

Our investigations concerning the nature of humility must include a reference to the signs of it or the various ways in which it is shown. That inward subjection of a human being to the Almighty, which has been mentioned as the essential element in the virtue, does not remain inward and no more. Like all the other virtues, it manifests itself and is seen in the conduct of life. "If we have interior humility, the body will naturally assume all the attitudes resulting from the reverence which fills the soul before God."[50] The presence of the virtue will be indicated by a gentleness of speaking, a quietness of features, a certain gravity of comportment. These things flow from the virtue that has been acquired.

[49] Marmion, *Christ, the Ideal of the Monk*, ch. 11.
[50] Ibid.

That is not all. They are also useful if the virtue has not been acquired, because they can help to produce it in us. Besides expressing it, they foster it. By means of them, therefore, we can with God's grace acquire humility. If these external acts of the virtue are often repeated, they have an effect on our soul; they gradually dispose our soul to be humble. It is a law of our nature that body affects soul and soul affects body.

There are so many acts of humility and — if practiced faithfully and discreetly, as they should be — they lead to the virtue itself.

Humility is acquired by two means: by the gift of grace and by human effort, but principally by grace. Thus it is that the inward virtue is present in us before the exterior signs appear, human effort being the means whereby we first restrain the outward signs of pride and then tear out its internal root.[51] By making an act of humility, we do not show that we are humble, but rather that we want to become humble. A humiliation is not a sign of humility already acquired, but, rather, of the will to acquire it.[52]

---

[51] *Summa Theologica*, II-II, Q. 161, art. 6.

[52] *Quaest. disp. de Perf. Evang.*, I.

The Power of Humility

With customary scientific precision, St. Thomas divides the outward signs of humility into three:

- *Actions:* we should keep to the common way and not act differently from others;

- *Words:* we should not speak before the proper time nor go beyond the mean in talking;

- *Gestures:* we should keep our eyes downcast and check the expression of foolish mirth.[53]

And St. Bonaventure tells us furthermore that a certain mean must be adhered to in these external acts. *Manliness* must be preserved in them, against the *pusillanimity* that degrades us. *Truth* must be observed, against the *hypocrisy* that deceives others. Finally, *propriety* must be maintained, against the *stolidity* that is unbecoming and stultifying.[54]

Happy are they who have eyes to see the workings of God that help us cultivate a humble spirit. Our whole time of probation here and the various humiliations that come our way are directed toward the repression of

---

[53] *Summa Theologica,* II-II, Q. 161, art. 6.

[54] *Quaest. disp. de Perf. Evang.,* I.

pride and the subjugation of our hearts to God and to His gifts, whether imparted to us or to our brethren. Never will it be known until the day of judgment what a prodigious amount of external and internal help God has given us, nor how numerous were all the occasions He provided to assist us in the exercise of humility. Never until that solemn day will it be known what an enormous provision of help and opportunity has been neglected.[55]

࿚

Pride and excessive self-depreciation
are both based on falsehood

Before finishing our study on the nature of humility, it will be useful — so as to throw the virtue into more distinct relief — to consider briefly the two vices opposed to it: self-depreciation and pride.

Self-depreciation, as we have seen, is the first act, the prime function, of humility. But it can also be a vice — that is, when carried too far. It must be clearly understood that there is one way in which self-depreciation cannot be carried too far, and this is in regard to our

---

[55] Ullathorne, *Groundwork of Christian Virtue*, 139.

dependence on the Lord. So essential is this dependence and so utter, that we cannot think too little of ourselves or lower ourselves too deeply. Self-depreciation before the Lord is most praiseworthy. Self-depreciation before our fellowmen can be overdone, though, and if it is excessive in our dealings with them, it becomes a vice. A moderate self-esteem is required for the good of others and for the correct fulfilling of our duties.

One of the deepest aspirations in a human being is to excel. It is a normal, healthy thing. When he follows this aspiration according to the light of Faith and the law of virtue, it leads him to true greatness of soul, to genuine excellence. But when he looks for excellence where it never is found (that is, in himself and not in God), he falls into pride. Pride is an immoderate desire to excel, a disorderly wish for our own greatness. The proud man has an exaggerated sense of his own importance, forgetting that all he is and all he has comes from God and belongs to God. Humility keeps to the rule of right reason, according to which a person has a true esteem of himself. The proud man violates this rule and thinks of himself things greater than really exist. This thinking arises from an irregular desire of his own excelling, because what we earnestly desire we easily believe.[56] On account of this immoderate wish, the will reaches out to and desires objects greater than are befitting. Whatever induces a person to think himself above what he is makes him fall into pride.

• Humility is founded on truth; pride on falsehood.

• Humility is correct self-depreciation; pride, improper self-exaltation.

• Humility recognizes our dependence on God; pride claims a spurious independence.

• Humility truthfully takes the lowest place; pride usurps the first place.

• Humility puts a man right with God; pride radically falsifies him.

But this much must be said in conclusion: there is a touch of subtlety in the virtue, for it would be no advantage to us to know that we possessed it. People who are humble do not like to be known as humble.

---

[56] *Summa Theologica*, II-II, Q. 162, art. 3.

Chapter Three

⚜

Why you need humility

All through the Sacred Book that has God for its Author — that series of love letters, as it has been called, which God sent to humanity — we are warned repeatedly against pride and bidden to cultivate humility. We have already seen our Lord's personal messages. But long before He came, it was an unceasing admonition: the prophets cry it out; the Psalms echo it; and the sapiential books[57] declare it again.

What the Lord accepts from man and what draws man near to Him is humility. What the Lord rejects and

---

[57] That is, Job, Psalms, Proverbs, Ecclesiastes, Canticles (Song of Solomon), Wisdom, and Ecclesiasticus (Sirach).

what turns man away from Him is pride. The blessings of God rain gently down upon the humble, while His wrath crashes about the heads of the proud.

Here are extracts from the Word of God. They should be read devoutly, for there is virtue in the prayerful reading of Sacred Scripture; it is then especially that the Word of God is "living and effectual."[58]

> *"He that hath been humbled shall be in glory:*
> *and he that shall bow down his eyes,*
> *he shall be saved."*
>
> Job 22:29

> *"Thou wilt save the humble people,*
> *but wilt bring down the eyes of the proud."*
>
> Ps. 17:28 (RSV = Ps. 18:27)

> *"The Lord is nigh unto them that are of a contrite heart:*
> *and He will save the humble of spirit."*
>
> Ps. 33:19 (RSV = Ps. 34:18)

> *"A contrite and humble heart,*
> *O God, Thou wilt not despise."*
>
> Ps. 50:19 (RSV = Ps. 51:17)

[58] Heb. 4:12.

Why you need humility

"I hate arrogance and pride
and every wicked way."
Prov. 8:13

"Where pride is there is also reproach,
but where humility is there also is wisdom."
Prov. 11:2

"Among the proud there are always contentions."
Prov. 13:10

"Humility goeth before glory."
Prov. 15:33

"Pride goeth before destruction."
Prov. 16:18

"The fruit of humility is the fear of the Lord,
riches and glory and life."
Prov. 22:4

"Seek not of the Lord a pre-eminence."
Ecclus. 7:4 (RSV = Sir. 7:4)

"The wisdom of the humble shall exalt his head
and shall make him sit in the midst of great men."
Ecclus. 11:1 (RSV = Sir. 11:1)

The Power of Humility

"The lofty eyes of men are humbled,
and the haughtiness of men shall be made to stoop:
and the Lord alone shall be exalted in that day."
Isa. 2:11

"Man shall be humbled,
and the eyes of the lofty
shall be brought low."
Isa. 5:15

"Be not proud, for the Lord hath spoken."
Jer. 13:15

"Thy arrogance hath deceived thee
and the pride of thy heart."
Jer. 49:16

"But when his heart was lifted up,
and his spirit hardened into pride,
he was put down from the throne of his kingdom,
and his glory was taken away."
Dan. 5:20

In the New Testament, written after our divine Lord had gone back to the Father, we find more messages from God:

Why you need humility

"*Put ye on, therefore, as the elect of God, holy and
beloved, mercy, benignity, humility, modesty, patience.*"
Col. 3:12

"*And do you all insinuate humility one to another.*"
1 Pet. 5:5

"*God resisteth the proud,
but to the humble He giveth grace.*"
1 Pet. 5:5; James 4:6

"*Be humbled in the sight of the Lord,
and He will exalt you.*"
James 4:10

" *. . . lest being puffed up with pride
he fall into the judgment of the Devil.*"
1 Tim. 3:6

"*He is proud, knowing nothing.*"
1 Tim. 6:4

"*For all that is in the world is the concupiscence
of the flesh, and the concupiscence of the eyes,
and the pride of life, which is not of the Father
but is of the world.*"
1 John 2:16

The Power of Humility

Remember that God resists the proud

Now, all Scripture is the heart of God, the mouth of God, the tongue of God, and the pen of God. Scripture is the mouth of the Father, the tongue of the Son, and the pen of the Holy Spirit.[59]

With this in mind, there is one divine message, quoted above, to which special attention must be given. Coming down to us from two apostles, it concerns pride. A strange statement, this is, from the pen of God. . . .[60] When we ponder it, we realize what grave need we have of humility.

God tells us that He *resists* the proud!

It is a dreadful thing for a man to be abandoned by God; he is graceless then and utterly derelict; he is left to his own puny self, in miserable isolation. But for God to be *active* against him, for a man to be the object of divine antagonism, is more dreadful still — a mortal opposed by almighty power; a man withstood by God.

There must be something most iniquitous, something radically hostile in pride for it to draw down on itself

---

[59] St. Bonaventure, *In Hex.*, XII.

[60] Cf. Marmion, *Christ, the Ideal of the Monk*, ch. 11.

God's antagonism. And indeed there is. The reason for this hatred springs from the very nature of God. He is the Source of whatever exists, the Cause of each and every perfection. He made all things and tells us that He made them for Himself.[61] Every creature must return to Him; to Him all glory must go.

In a human being this would be the greatest selfishness, but it is not so in the Deity. If we apply the term *selfishness* to Him, it has no meaning. God cannot do anything except for Himself. It would be contradictory to His nature to act otherwise. God would cease to be God if He acted for any purpose outside Himself. He would be subjecting Himself to a finite thing, and there would be self-contradiction in the subordination of the infinite to the finite.

St. John says that he saw in a vision on Patmos the blessed prostrating themselves before the throne of the Most High and repeating, "Thou art worthy, O Lord our God, to receive honor and glory and power: because Thou hast created all things; and for Thy will they were and have been created."[62]

[61] Prov. 16:4.
[62] Apoc. 4:11 (RSV = Rev. 4:11).

The Power of Humility

God Himself has declared that He will not give His glory to another.[63] He cannot, for, in contemplating Himself, He sees that an infinite glory is due to Him because of the fullness of His being and His infinite perfections.

He gives us, it is true, His only Son; He gives us many graces; He gives us eternal life; He deigns to give us, through the Holy Spirit, an intimate fellowship with the Most Blessed Trinity. But one thing He neither will nor can give to others: the glory proper to Himself.

This is what the proud man endeavors to appropriate. He tries to take what belongs uniquely to God, to steal the glory that is God's alone. Theoretically he might know that everything comes from God, but he behaves as if it came from himself. The evil of pride consists largely in trying to deprive God of the divine attribute whereby He is the First Beginning and the Last End. It is an unjust aggression, and it sets up an antagonism between man and God. God cannot help but resist him.

We see, therefore, that the proud man fails in a leading duty, in the primary purpose of his existence: the rendering of glory to his Creator. He cannot sincerely say, "Glory be to the Father and to the Son and to the

---

[63] Isa. 42:8.

Holy Spirit." To put the matter in a sentence: God is all; man is nothing. Pride endeavors to make man something, and in the attempt there is an essential falseness, a going against the facts.

When, however, we put away the foolishness of pride and admit that of ourselves we are helpless and sinful, we implicitly acknowledge the power and goodness of God. We pay homage to His perfection, and God is so pleased that He stoops, as it were, to our humility and fills us with His gifts. His gaze rests benignly upon us, for Scripture tells us that His regard is for the humble: "The Lord is high and looketh on the low."[64]

Furthermore, when through frailty we are deficient in some virtue, if we humble ourselves before God, our humility actually compensates for our other deficiencies. God is propitiated by lowliness.

⽊

Humility is the foundation of all virtues
It would be an error to think that humility is the most excellent of the virtues. The theological virtues — faith, hope, and charity — are far superior; so are justice and

---

[64] Ps. 137:6 (RSV = Ps. 138:6).

the intellectual virtues. But inasmuch as it is the *basis* of every virtue, humility is first. From it, all the virtues begin; through it, they grow; in it, they are perfected; and by it, they are maintained. All these virtues may be compared to an edifice; the first thing done to build them may be likened to the foundation. Humility is that necessary foundation. It holds first place among the virtues insofar as it removes pride, makes a man subject, and prepares him to receive the gift of divine grace. Our Lord recommends it insistently because it most effectively clears away the one obstacle to human salvation.[65]

"The sure road that leads to God," says St. Augustine, "is first humility, next humility, and lastly humility. Ask me the question as often as you may; my answer will ever be the same. There are other precepts in God's Law, but unless humility precede and follow our good works and also accompany them . . . unless we hold fast to it and repress pride and all vain self-conceit, our good deeds will be snatched out of our hands. . . . Pride lurks even in our good actions and must be guarded against, lest it rob us of our merit."[66]

---

[65] *Summa Theologica*, II-II, Q. 161, art. 5.
[66] Quoted in *Quaest. disp. de Perf. Evang.*, I.

No light can reach us from Heaven, no charity can enter the soul, unless humility is there to prepare the way. It opens the soul to the doctrine of Christ and the heart to His grace. When a man is humble, God bestows grace upon him; and the humbler he is, the higher God will raise him in grace and the more peace He will impart.

As the *Imitation of Christ* says, "The humble man God protects and delivers; the humble He loves and comforts; to the humble He inclines Himself; to the humble He gives grace and, after he has been lowered, raises him to glory. To the humble He reveals His secrets, and sweetly draws and invites him to Himself. . . . Never think thou hast made any progress till thou look upon thyself as inferior to all."[67]

• *Faith.* Pride makes belief in Christianity impossible. Humility is indispensable for faith. The humble man alone can believe, because blinding pride has been banished from his heart and God has entered and enkindled in its place the first of the virtues — faith.

St. Paul draws attention to the fundamentalness of belief in Christ. "Other foundation no man can lay than

[67] *Imitation of Christ*, Bk. 2, ch. 2, no. 2.

that which is laid, which is Christ Jesus."[68] Faith has priority. For a mortal desiring to have access to God, faith is the primary positive thing. "He that cometh to God must believe. . . ."[69] In a manner nobler than humility, it is the foundation of the other virtues.[70] Humility prepares a man for God; it is the *negative* foundation. Faith puts him into contact with God; it is the *positive* foundation. It is the bowing down of our mind to a supernatural truth that we do not understand. We assent to it on the authority of God, who has revealed it. The proud man will reject what he fails to comprehend; his pride will prevent him from believing. Hence, pride of mind is one of the most dangerous vices.

Humility is necessary, not merely for Christian belief, but for each of the virtues in turn. It is an element present in every one of them, and without it none can be acquired. For this reason, it has been called a *universal* virtue.

• *Hope*. In the theological habit of hope you find humility. Besides being a firm expectation of the happiness

[68] 1 Cor. 3:11.

[69] Heb. 11:6.

[70] *Summa Theologica*, II-II, Q. 161, art. 5.

of Heaven, hope relies on God to supply the means of reaching that happiness. It is a state of dependence on the divine assistance. The self-sufficiency of pride would prevent such dependence. Only the humble man relies on God; in himself or in his own efforts he places not the slightest confidence, knowing himself too well for that.

We must remember that utter self-distrust, with an unfailing reliance on the Lord, is the very ABC of spirituality. Unless we direct all our prayers and efforts toward acquiring this attitude, we shall make no progress. Rather, our rashness and unwarranted self-reliance will result in many shameful falls. God will use them to punish us. For He realizes it is not enough that we know our helplessness; He wants us to be thoroughly persuaded of it.

The thoughtful person will, in addition, try to cultivate a consciousness of dependence on the Immaculate Mother of God. Through her maternal hands, all graces come down from the Father of Mercies to men. Children always rely on their mother.

• *Charity.* That great figure in sacred history, St. Benedict,[71] whose rule is almost entirely a treatise on

---

[71] St. Benedict (c. 480-c. 547), abbot; father of Western monasticism.

humility, informs us that he who practices this virtue will arrive at the perfection of charity. This promise shows that there must be a relation between humility and the greatest of all the virtues. We see it clearly when we reflect that during all our years of probation in this world, it will be a case of the terrific alternative: God or self. Either we love God or we love self. The characteristic of the lost is their rejection of everything that is not self. This inordinate love of self is the cause of pride. It renders charity impossible. The heart of the proud cannot at all receive the charity of God, for pride repels God. No man who is full of himself has room for God. But when we have emptied ourselves, God will be able to fill us. When we make room for Him, He will come, as He has promised through two of His apostles: "God giveth his grace to the humble."[72] No wonder St. Peter adds to that statement the exhortation "Be you humbled, therefore, under the mighty hand of God."[73]

Our Lord tells us of one man to whose lowliness God came with His grace and His charity. It was the publican who prayed in the Temple, crying for mercy on his sins,

[72] James 4:6; 1 Pet. 5:5.
[73] 1 Pet. 5:6.

whose prayer pierced the clouds, and who went back to his home "justified"[74] — that is, restored to sanctifying grace and charity. "Through humility," says St. Thomas, "sin is forgiven."[75]

Scripture tells us that pride is hateful not only to God but also to men.[76] The proud man finds the practice of fraternal charity impossible, for his arrogance and conceit are the cause of many clashes with his fellows. He is always ready to take offense. His selfishness violates the rights of others. But to the humble man the observance of charity is easy. He claims no rights for himself, never questions the rights of others, and always gives God and men their due. In him are courtesy, respect, considerateness, mortification — all of which are involved in the fulfilling of the precept of fraternal love. It is obvious that for charity toward our neighbor, humility is required. St. Augustine assures us that "we cannot attain to charity except through humility."

‧ *Chastity*. Although the relation between humility and chastity is not so apparent, it is there. At Port-Royal

---

[74] Luke 18:14.

[75] *Summa Theologica*, II-II, Q. 161, art. 5.

[76] Ecclus. 10:7 (RSV = Sir. 10:7).

The Power of Humility

there was a convent of nuns in which monastic disci-
pline was not well maintained. Reports reached the
Holy See, with the result that a papal visitor was ap-
pointed. After holding the visitation, he reported that
the religious were "pure as angels, but proud as devils."
A great modern authority on the spiritual life has remarked that this report had little meaning, for nobody
could be pure and proud at the same time. Indeed God
often allows persons to fall into sins of the flesh to punish their pride. This is what St. Paul refers to when he
speaks of men "who became vain in their thoughts"
and, professing themselves to be wise, they became
fools, "who changed the truth of God into a lie." "And
as they liked not to have God in their knowledge, God
delivered them up to a reprobate sense so that they do
what is not fitting."[77]

But the point is that only the humble man will in
self-distrust avoid what he knows to be a danger to chastity. Only he will appeal to God for help when tempted.
It is a matter of daily experience that such temptations
are overcome by praying to our Lady and by making acts
of humility.

[77] Rom. 1:21, 25, 28 (Confraternity translation).

• *Prayer.* Prayer is an all-important exercise of the virtue of religion. Many theological and devotional tracts have been written on it, and no subject has been more thoroughly studied by learned and holy minds. They have accurately described how we should use this key to Heaven so as to order our lives properly and attain to lasting happiness. But God Himself emphasizes one condition and stresses one element in the true method of praying. He reminds us, "The prayer of him that humbleth himself shall pierce the clouds."[78] "To whom shall I have respect but to him that is poor and little, and of a contrite heart, and that trembleth at my words?"[79] "The prayer of the humble and meek hath always pleased God."[80] "He hath had regard to the prayer of the humble, and He hath not despised their petition."[81] "To him that is little, mercy is granted."[82]

The emphasis on the one note, the single quality, shows that what is necessary above all is that prayer be

---

[78] Ecclus. 35:21 (RSV = Sir. 35:17).

[79] Isa. 66:2.

[80] Cf. Jth. 9:16.

[81] Ps. 101:18 (RSV = Ps. 102:17).

[82] Wisd. 6:7.

The Power of Humility

humble. If that element be present, the remaining qualities of correct prayer will be there too. There is no other way of addressing the Almighty than in humility. Nor is there any other way of living our life.

Deep in the nature of prayer we find humility. On analysis it will be seen that prayer is essentially an act of subjection, something done only by him who is in due subjection. The proud man does not know his fundamental weakness, nor does he know his constant need of grace; hence, he does not pray for assistance, or else he prays without conviction. But the humble man adores God — that is, he admits his full dependence on his Maker. He asks God to give him what is necessary for soul and body, and again he thereby admits his dependence. He thanks God for all he has received, but gratitude also is an avowal of dependence. He atones for his treatment of God — reparation, too, is an act of subjection. True prayer is an exercise of the virtue of humility.

• *Reception of graces*. St. Teresa of Avila[83] tells us that she could not recall having received any notable mercy except when she found herself, as it were, annihilated

[83] St. Teresa of Avila (1515-1582), Spanish Carmelite nun and mystic.

at the sight of her sins. Her illustrious namesake, St. Thérèse of Lisieux, whom Pius XI has called the greatest saint of our age, says, "Things needful should be asked for with humility, as the poor stretch out their hands, hoping to get what is necessary; if refused, they are not astonished: no one owes them anything." By grace her mind was opened to see a meaning in the incident recorded in St. Luke's Gospel. The Apostles had spent the whole night in their boat, fishing. Their efforts were unsuccessful. But when they had acknowledged their powerlessness, they succeeded in landing a very great catch. "Perhaps," St. Thérèse remarked, "if they had taken a *few little fishes*, the Master would not have worked a miracle; but they had nothing, and so by the divine power and goodness their nets were soon filled with great fishes. That is just His way: He gives as God, but *He will have humility of heart*."[84]

There is no need to go through each of the various virtues; suffice it to say that humility is the precursor of them all. Even as the Baptist prepared the hearts of men to receive their Savior, so this virtue prepares our heart

---

[84] St. Thérèse of Lisieux (1873-1897; Carmelite nun), *Letter to Céline*, October 1893.

to receive the Savior's graces and virtues. It is a disposition of soul that facilitates our free access to spiritual and divine goods.[85] More than any other virtue, it puts our soul into readiness for those divine gifts which unite us to God. This is what Marmion calls the sublime recompense of humility.[86]

Christ was born in a cave. The shepherds who went to Bethlehem to see Him had to stoop to enter the cave. It was then "they found Mary and Joseph and the Infant lying in the manger."[87] Like the shepherds, every man has to stoop in order to come to Mary and her divine Son. The stoop is humility. The humble man alone can draw near to Christ, and the closer he approaches, the humbler he must be.

The need and importance of humility are beyond doubt, considering that it is the foundation of all the virtues. Without it, we cannot acquire or maintain any of them. Until we are perfectly humble, some insincerity will lurk in all our virtue. It is not surprising to hear the Seraphic Doctor call humility the sum total of

[85] *Summa Theologica*, II-II, Q. 161, art. 5.

[86] Marmion, *Christ, the Ideal of the Monk*, ch. 11.

[87] Luke 2:16.

perfection and the way of salvation. "If one leaves it, he is lost. If one exalts himself even a little more than he ought, he is in danger. As St. Bernard says, 'If a man raises his head on entering through a door, he is injured; but if he stoops, he escapes injury.' Therefore, Blessed Anthony was assured that only the humble man can avoid the snares of the Devil."[88]

We possess holiness only insofar as we possess humility. The degree of our holiness is the same as the degree of our grace; and in the identical measure that we have grace, we have humility, because grace is given only to the humble. It is impossible to imagine a true Christian lacking this virtue, or a perfect Christian who has not a high degree of it.

And so we are forced to the conclusion that unless a humble dependence on God is the mainstay of our life, we must have serious misgiving about the state in which God will find our souls at the hour of death.

[88] St. Bonaventure, *In Hex.*, coll. 1.

Chapter Four

Remember who you really are

Assuredly there are many reasons for a human being to be humble, and so compelling are they that St. Thomas — possibly the greatest intellect the world has ever known — was at a loss to understand how anyone could be proud. Among these reasons, there are the sins by which we have offended the Lord. But they are not the first reason. We have already stated that man of himself is *nothing*. There you have the primary ground for humility. We must now carefully consider the truth of this statement; and again our reading must be mingled with a prayer that God in His mercy may impress deeply upon us the knowledge of our nothingness, for on this knowledge, let it be repeated, the virtue depends for its existence.

The Power of Humility

The human mind can prove — and God has revealed — that God *created* the universe, man included.
That is, He has caused it to be, has made it out of no
pre-existing material. In the eternity previous to creation, there was outside of God the void of nothingness,
the emptiness of non-existence. God was alone; solely
the Deity existed in unutterable perfection. "I am who
am," He says.[89] It is only He who is being, whose nature
it is to exist. By an act of the almighty will, man came
into being from non-existence. This is why God has
warned man of his origin: "If any man think himself to
be something, *whereas he is nothing,* he deceives himself."[90] Man, then, is not something of himself; he deceives himself if he considers that he is. Of himself he
was nothing and would simply remain non-existent. The
pagan philosopher Plato says that no being truly exists
but God. But from untold millions of potential beings
the Lord chose us for existence, without our having any
possible right or merit to live. You who read these lines,
and he who pens them, must bear in mind that we need
not be and that we have not deserved to be.

[89] Exod. 3:14.
[90] Gal. 6:3.

Now, it would be a mistake to think of creation as an act of God that is finished. The act is continuous. God is always creating. He did not, so to speak, put His hand to the work and then withdraw, leaving the work independent of Himself (as would a sculptor whose task is ended and whose statue stands by itself). No, God must go on keeping His work in being — which is but another way of saying that He continues creating what He has created.

This idea must be well understood. It is essential if we wish to realize how radical is our dependence on God. We must not think of creation as over and done with, but rather as an operation from which God never for an instant desists. The fact that the universe perdures and that we continue to live is due to this uninterrupted process of creating. Were God to cease from the act, were He to cease upholding us in being, we would immediately lapse back into the nothingness from which we were drawn.

Somewhat of an analogy is found in the action of a man regarding himself in a mirror. He sees his own image. But if he withdraws from the glass, his image straightway vanishes; it no longer exists. So it is with God and us. If God were to withdraw His creative power, we would vanish utterly. Not that we would die; we would simply cease to be, without a trace. It is therefore quite plain that we depend on God, and on God only — entirely, always, and essentially. This dependence is so profound that nobody could continue to exist for one moment without God's conserving him.

"When we use," says Fr. Faber, "the words *dependence, submission, helplessness* . . . about our relation to God, we are using words which, inasmuch as they express also certain relations in which we may stand to our fellow-creatures, are really inadequate to express our position toward our Creator. We have no one word which can fully convey . . . the utterness of that honorable abjection in which we lie before Him who made us."[91]

Since of himself man is nothing and has nothing, it follows that man has received and now receives from God alone all that he possesses. By the continuous action of God, all that man is, all that man has, and all that man can do is preserved for him. It must have been considerations such as these that made St. Paul ask the famous question: "What hast thou that thou hast not received? And if thou hast received, why dost thou

[91] Frederick William Faber, *Creature and Creator*, 56.

glory as if thou hadst not received?"[92] It was not the first time the query was put. Long years before that, the Lord had inquired of man, "Why is earth and ashes proud?"[93] No reply has ever been made. The *why* is unanswerable, because pride cannot give any reason for its existence, founded as it is on falsehood. It is a lie being lived, the most uncreaturely of the vices, a practical disregard of our complete dependence on God.

In some Franciscan communities, a prayer is said on Friday evenings: "Lord Jesus Christ, we are nothing; we can do nothing; we are worth nothing; badly do we serve Thee; we are unprofitable servants. Lord Jesus Christ, have mercy on us." This prayer expresses some of the reasons we have for being humble.

ༀ

You cannot perform a good action without God

So far, we have been devoting attention to our nothingness from the viewpoint of our total dependence on God for existence and all that goes with it. And we see that it is a potent reason for humbling ourselves "under

[92] 1 Cor. 4:7.
[93] Ecclus. 10:9 (RSV = Sir. 10:9).

the mighty hand of God." But ours is a nothingness under another very important aspect.

Man of himself is nothing in the order of nature. And nothing either in the order of grace. We have our Lord's word on man's absolute powerlessness in this realm. "Without me you can do nothing."[94] No teaching of the Redeemer must be better noted. Let us reflect on the truth of it.

The elevating of a creature to sanctifying grace is a gratuitous act of God. In no wise did He owe it to man. The very name *grace* is related to the word *gratis,* something given freely. It is a wholly undeserved gift granted in consideration of the merits of Christ. To Him who came on earth that we might be elevated to grace and have abundant life[95] we should be humbly grateful. For sanctifying grace is something wonderful, tremendous — a supernatural quality that comes from God and affects the soul, not changing but modifying the substance of it. God rarely uses superlatives, but He calls grace "most great and precious."[96] It is life, the divine life, a sharing

[94] John 15:5.
[95] John 10:10.
[96] 2 Pet. 1:4.

by men in the very life that is in our Lord Himself. Think of it as a nature, completely above our own nature, entirely undue to it, and (be it remarked) completely above the nature even of angels. It is supernatural in the full sense of the term. When raised to it, man is a partaker of the divine nature.

The thought fills us with confusion. This sublime state, and our undeservingness all the more, should make us humble ourselves.

But we cannot yet perform any act that will bring us a reward in Heaven. Even though we are in the state of grace, a meritorious deed is still beyond us. Sanctifying grace is a nature. According to it we act. But it does not *make* us act; it does not excite the will to perform a deed. We require it, but we require something else as well. To do the smallest meritorious act, we need God enlightening our mind and moving our will. We begin to see why our Lord said, "Without me you can do nothing" — especially when we realize that we need another distinct grace, besides sanctifying grace, to perform the tiniest supernatural action. Without this additional help, we cannot act. We need certain lights from God to *show our mind* the good to be done and certain inward motions to *move our will* to do it. This we call *actual grace*. If we cooperate with it, we can perform the meritorious deed.

Still, that is not all. The full truth of our Lord's words dawns on us when we learn that we need a particular grace even to cooperate. Cooperation with grace is itself a grace. Exactly how our free will is moved is a mystery — one that shows how utterly dependent we are.

And so in the world of the supernatural, ours is an innate and absolute helplessness without God. Lacking His grace, neither thought nor word nor any deed of ours — nothing on our part — avails for Heaven. This truth has been defined by the Church as an article of Faith. "For it is God who worketh in you both to will and to accomplish,"[97] and "No man can say, 'Jesus is Lord' save in the Holy Spirit."[98]

It is true that when, by this indispensable heavenly help, we have performed a good action in sanctifying grace, we acquire a strict right to a reward hereafter. This is what is meant by a meritorious act. But if the very merit of what we do is our own, it is so just because God allows us to merit. Our merits are *His gifts*. Let us listen

[97] Phil. 2:13.
[98] Cf. 1 Cor. 12:3.

to the Council of Trent: "Far be it from the Christian man to trust or glory in himself and not in the Lord. The Lord's goodness is so great toward all men that those things which are His gifts He wills to be their merits."[99]

All this is cumulative evidence of our complete ineffectualness in the order of grace. When we realize our incompetence, we see immediately that self-depreciation is the logical and correct course of action, and that self-exaltation or self-glorification is wild and most absurd. When we reflect on this aspect of our nothingness, we humble ourselves before the great God to whom we owe so much — to whom we owe everything. St. Thomas said that the essence of humility consists in a certain praiseworthy abasing of self to the last degree. We have ample reason indeed to humble ourselves to the dust. Christ's words come to mind again: "But when thou art invited, go, sit down in the lowest place."[100] This taking of the last seat is truth in action.

A thought may present itself: we may consider it impossible to understand that we are of ourselves mere nothingness. Experience somehow appears to be against

[99] Sess. 6, ch. 16.
[100] Luke 14:10.

it. It is plain to us that actually we *are something* and that we *can do something*. How then . . . ? Or the idea may occur: how can we consider ourselves the greatest sinner when we know others who have done worse?

We are warned that such thoughts are foreign to the virtue and should be a matter for self-reproach. We are still far from genuine humility if we think we can fully grasp the truth of our being nil. The truly humble man believes that of himself he is mere nothingness and a greater sinner than others. He knows this is true, although he does not care to investigate how it is true. He has practical knowledge of it. He may be unable to explain it to others, but he is as unconcerned about this as he is about his inability to explain how he sees with his eyes.[101]

"Real wisdom it is," says St. Bonaventure, "to recognize truly one's own nothingness and the sublimity of God."[102] We must observe that he speaks of recognizing it *truly*. That we are absolutely nothing of ourselves and that we are sheerly dependent on the Lord are facts, even if we never were aware of them. But facts can be

[101] Cf. Cajetan Mary da Bergamo, *Humility of Heart*, trans. Herbert Cardinal Vaughan (Westminster, Maryland: The Newman Press, 1944), 120-121.

[102] *Quaest. disp. de Perf. Evang.*, I.

treated in different ways. A man can turn his back on them and ignore them. This is how the proud behave; their conduct is entirely at variance with the facts. Or a man can see the truth of them after a fashion and do little about them, as happens with those who are not very proud and still not really humble. Or a man can recognize them *truly*, as the humble man does. Because he really recognizes that alone he is nothing, in nature or grace, he behaves accordingly. Since the facts are there, he deems himself to be of no account. The recognition is genuine only when activity is in keeping with it.

Man's native nothingness and many other motives may be indicated as a reason for humility, but no one reason, nor all the reasons brought forward, will produce it in us. We must ponder the matter well and, above all, pray earnestly. Then God in His goodness will bestow the gift, the grace of self-knowledge, on which the virtue is based. To be practically aware of our nothingness and our powerlessness is a grace, one of the greatest that the Lord can give. "Not that we are sufficient to think anything of ourselves, as of ourselves: but our sufficiency is from God."[103] Only after much prayer

[103] 2 Cor. 3:5.

will a person be able, like Jeremiah the prophet, to say truly, "I am the man that sees my poverty."[104]

The Seraphic Doctor, noting our twofold nothingness (that is, in the natural and supernatural orders), explains that humility is consequently twofold.[105] There is the humility of truth, which comes from the consideration of our nothingness as regards nature. This is found even among the angels and the blessed. And there is the humility of severity, which comes from the consideration of our guilt.

❦

Considering your sins should make you humbler

We have reason to be humble when we think of our sins. Although not the primary reason for the virtue, our sins afford the greatest ground for it. Indeed we are told that one of the chief reasons we lack humility is that we too readily forget the sins we have committed.

It is helpful to recall St. Thomas's distinction of the two things that may be considered in man: that whatever makes for salvation and perfection in man is of

[104] Lam. 3:1.
[105] *Quaest. disp. de Perf. Evang.*, I.

God, and that whatever there is of fault in him belongs to man himself. Consequently, if there be any good in us, it must be ascribed entirely to God, for to Him alone it is due. We are left with our sins; they are our own, something we have not received from God, the only thing we can claim as our own, the only thing we have of ourselves and which must be ascribed to ourselves. The cause of sin is our depraved will.

The publican in the Temple thought of his sins. The sorrowful memory made him strike his breast and dare not lift up his eyes, but humbly implore mercy from the Lord: "O God, be merciful to me, a sinner."[106] The thought of his sins led him to humility. So will it be with us. If we but remember our sins, we shall never be proud. And as we turn our thoughts back to the years that are dead, and recall the many times, the repeated occasions, that we offended the Lord both mortally and venially, it becomes abundantly clear that we have much reason to humble ourselves down to earth, abase ourselves to the lowest, and crave the divine mercy. If we have *only once* in our life sinned gravely, we have deserved to be thrown out into "exterior darkness" where the eternal

[106] Luke 18:13.

gloom is filled with the noise of "weeping and gnashing of teeth."[107] Such would be our fate in strict justice. And if God has not cast us away from His face, but rather has pardoned our offense, it is due entirely to His infinite goodness. "The mercies of the Lord that we are not consumed."[108] The Church, in one of her collects, makes us admit that we are destitute of every virtue, and yet we esteem ourselves so excessively that we are troubled if others do not esteem us also.[109] This is due to a failure in remembering our sins and a resultant lack of proper self-knowledge.

There is something fearfully mysterious in human transgressions, for the psalmist asks. "Who can understand sins?"[110] What man can measure the infinite offense he gives to the All-Holy or estimate the enormous outrage he inflicts on the Divine Majesty? What man will ever know the deep anguish he causes to the Sacred Heart of our blessed Lord, who died for us — an anguish that is shared by the Immaculate Heart of His Mother?

---

[107] Matt. 8:12.

[108] Lam. 3:22.

[109] Collect, Second Sunday of Lent.

[110] Ps. 18:13 (RSV = Ps. 19:12).

On the sinner's side, however, there is nothing of mystery about sin: what it is, and what its effects are, are fully known. A mortal offense is a great disorder, a complete turning away from God, our Last End. When the act is done, it leaves us in a state of aversion from God. Our soul is stained by the sin, deprived of sanctifying grace.

We began life, as we know, with a nature wounded by Original Sin; but by our own personal misdeeds, it is again deformed. Our nature is doubly vitiated. In addition to the bad effects of Adam's Fall, our own sins have strengthened our inclination to evil, increased the darkness of our intellect, and further hardened our will. Our Lord told us of these severe injuries when He said, "For the heart of this people is grown gross, and with their ears they have been dull of hearing, and their eyes they have shut."[111]

Sinners we are and objects of the mercy of God. No amount of forgiveness can alter this fact. Even at present, there are the many sins into which we fall, day after day, by word and thought and action — the many offenses we commit against God and our fellowman. They

[111] Matt. 13:15.

are venial, it is true, but numerous and at times fully voluntary — and that, too, in spite of all God has done for us, the graces and the lights He has given us. The great danger of these sins is that they lessen the reverential fear we should have of God and deprive us of the special helps and graces we so sorely need.

We know for certain that we have sinned, but are not so certain that our guilt is now removed. In fact, we can never be absolutely sure that it is. A well-known Scripture text reminds us, "Man knows not whether he be worthy of love or hatred."[112]

St. Paul, as a mortal, had the unique privilege of being rapt up into the Third Heaven.[113] Nevertheless he said, "I am not conscious to myself of anything, yet am I not hereby justified."[114] Even though his conscience did not reproach him, he could not be sure that he was in the state of grace. What assurance can *we* have then? "Be not without fear about sin forgiven, and add not sin to sin."[115]

---

[112] Eccles. 9:1.
[113] 2 Cor. 12:2.
[114] 1 Cor. 4:4.
[115] Cf. Ecclus. 5:5 (RSV = Sir. 5:5).

If we ask ourselves whether it is possible that we should ever again commit a mortal sin after being pardoned by our Lord and after all the various helps we have gotten from Him, in honesty we must reply that it is quite possible. For through our own fault, our inclination to it is greater than it previously was. If God takes away His hand from us, we are certain of doing what we did before, and worse. Let God remove His grace, and immediately we fall. The prayer of St. Philip Neri[116] was "Lord, keep Thy hand over Philip today, for if Thou dost not, Philip will betray Thee." And St. Francis of Assisi used to say, "If any criminal had received as much of God's mercy as I, he would be ten times more spiritual than I."

⁕

Consider what you were, what you are,
and what you may become

What has been said can now be summed up in three points that form a useful exercise for fostering humility in our heart. Consider what you *were*, what you *are*, and

---

[116] St. Philip Neri (1515-1595), Italian priest; founder of the Congregation of the Oratory.

what you *may become*. Acknowledge the full extent of your past miseries, your present unworthiness, and the possibility of future infidelity.

• *What you were:* A few years ago, you were non-existent, and of yourself you would remain so. Your utter nothingness of yourself should make you truly deem yourself as of no account. The remembrance of your past sins, imputable to you alone, should give you a most abject notion of what you were; the manner in which you treated God should make you despise yourself. If others slight you, the thought of your sins will enable you to bear it; it is very little for your sins.

• *What you are:* You cannot take one step toward God without Him; you are incapable of a good thought without His grace. You offend God by your present daily infidelities and your ingratitude. Your best actions are very faulty.

• *What you may become:* The source of your past sins still exists in you. It gave rise to them before, and it can do so again. The same cause produces the same effects. Unless God gives you grace, you are fully capable of relapsing and of becoming even worse than you were. How can you be proud?[117]

These considerations are somber but salutary. They should, however, be illumined with another thought. Always there is the boundless mercy of God, the infinite merits of the Savior, and the confident intercession of our Lady in Heaven.[118] It is most comforting to know that if our offenses are ours, the merits of Christ's life and Passion are also ours, for He has made them over to us and, in His goodness, has willed that His Blessed Mother should always plead with gentle assurance on our behalf. In spite of our unworthiness, we should throw ourselves upon God, confident in His mercy and in the merits of His Son, certain that He cannot repel us. Never do we glorify God more than when we do so.[119]

---

[117] Cf. Raymond Thibaut, *Abbot Columba Marmion*, trans. Mother Mary St. Thomas (St. Louis: B. Herder, 1932), 103.

[118] Cf. Secret for the vigil of the Assumption.

[119] Cf. Thibault, *Abbot Columba Marmion*, 103.

Chapter Five

જ્જ

Learn humility
from our Lord

Not without cause has our Lord said, "Learn of me, for I am meek and humble of heart."[120] It is because He is humble that we are invited to learn. His humility is one of His attractions, drawing us to copy Him. No more efficacious remedy can be found for the ravagings of our pride than to place before our eyes the humility of Christ.[121] It is a remedy for the vice and a reason for the virtue — the next point, therefore, that we shall consider. It affords a most important ground for humility in

[120] Matt. 11:29.

[121] De Blois, quoted by Marmion, *Christ, the Ideal of the Monk.*

this way: that resemblance to our Lord is imperative if we wish to be saved. God has preordained that we should be "made conformable to the image of His Son."[122]

Therefore, in all Christians there must necessarily be a Christlikeness. Because Christ was humble, we should be humble.

And more perhaps than any other virtue, humility makes us resemble our Lord. It would seem to be the one virtue in Him that is most described. It is constantly referred to, as though the men who had lived with Him marveled at it even more than at His raising the dead to life.

But first let us review the theological principles concerned. In the Redeemer there are two natures: that of God and that of man. These two natures are united in His divine Person. It is the Second Person in the Most Adorable Trinity who is God and who is at the same time man. *As God*, Christ could not be humble — that is, according to the full meaning of the term. If the virtue, as we have seen, springs from reverence toward the Godhead and if it essentially consists in due subjection to the Lord, it is obvious that only a creature can possess

[122] Rom. 8:29.

the virtue and that God cannot be humble in the sense in which angels and men can. "Humility does not belong to God according to His divine nature."[123]

But *as man*, Christ could and did exercise humility in a certain most wonderful way. "Christ knew His own excellence and impeccability from the union of the Word and that therefore He was worthy of all honor. He could not esteem Himself as of no account. But His most holy humanity knew that it was received from God and that if it were deserted by the Divinity, it would lapse into ignorance and into proneness toward sin. For this reason He was humble, profoundly subject to the Divinity, and referred to it all the honor shown to Him."[124]

⚜

Christ humbled Himself in His Incarnation

St. Paul advises us to be of one mind with our Lord, and in a very notable phrase he describes the humility of the Savior: "He emptied Himself."[125]

---

[123] *Summa Theologica*, II-II, Q. 161, art. 1.

[124] Billuart, *Tract. de Coet. Virt.*, 205.

[125] Phil. 2:7.

The Power of Humility

As we contemplate this humility, we stand before the most amazing revelation of the virtue that the mind of angel or man can conceive. The Pauline idea of it may be rendered thus: "Although He was God and possessed all the glory that belongs to God, He did not regard that glory as something which should at all costs be retained. He put it aside; He allowed it to be obscured in the lowliness of human existence; He emptied Himself out by taking the form of a slave, which occurred in the Incarnation."[126]

Our Lord's knowledge, as man, surpasses that of all the saints; far better than they, He knows the immeasurable distance between Creator and creature. He knows how far down He came when He, the Creator, became a human creature. Man is far below God, infinitely beneath Him. Only the Son of God is aware of the unlimited distance He had to travel to reach the estate of man. If humility is a lowering of self, then as you kneel at the crib before the little newborn Infant, the eternal Father's Almighty Word who leapt down from His royal throne,[127]

---

[126] Patrick Boylan, *The Sunday Epistles and Gospels*, "Palm Sunday."

[127] Cf. Wisd. 18:15.

you can in some poor manner realize how He has low-ered Himself and what a long journey He has made to appear in such condition.

Even as a Babe, He knew perfectly the divine dignity of His Person and the sovereign respect and adoration due to Him. Hence, He felt all the more the extreme humiliations He had to endure in the lowliness of hu-man existence. You must recall the circumstances of His birth, the dark and damp cave in the hillside, the swad-dling clothes, the homage of the poor shepherds com-ing in to Him from the fields at midnight. "Lying He was in the manger and in Heaven He was shining."[128] "You must hear the small inarticulate cry from His in-fant lips; you must see the little limbs atremble with the chill of the cave, and Mary the Virgin-Mother ador-ing profoundly the eternity of Him who was but a min-ute old."[129] These things we must ponder if we would appreciate, however inadequately, the extent of the di-vine self-emptying.

That God became man is a doctrine well known to Christians. The very familiarity of the words may blur

[128] Breviary.
[129] Frederick William Faber, *Bethlehem*, 154.

their significance, but they enshrine what St. Thomas did not hesitate to call "the miracle of miracles." For the Deity to become a human being, for a Man who was God to walk this earth, for a Person who was at once the Almighty and our fellowman to move about among us implies a condescension whose extent will never be measured, a stooping down from a height that will never be fully known, an act of humility whose depths will never be plumbed.

As long as the world lasts, the mind of man will be filled with amazement at the sight of the Omnipotent on a little bed of straw.

The Incarnation was truly an act of supreme self-humiliation on the part of the Son of God, and His whole life on earth was one long series of humiliations in harmony with the initial act whereby "the Word was made flesh."[130] When the ruler greeted Him as "good Master," He replied, "Why dost thou call me good? None is good but God alone."[131] The honor shown Him as man was referred immediately to the Divinity. For Himself as man He disclaimed everything. He spoke of

---

[130] John 1:14.
[131] Luke 18:18-19.

"the works that I do in the name of my Father,"[132] letting us see that it was in the name of the Father that He acted. He constantly ascribed all His works to His eternal Father. "I cannot of myself do anything."[133] "I do nothing of myself, but as the Father hath taught me, those things I speak."[134] It is indeed plain that our Lord lived in total and continuous subjection to God. And this, we must remember, is the essence of humility. As man, He is filled with reverence toward His Father. This reverence sprang from the knowledge of His own nothingness as a human being. He beheld the superexcellence and immense majesty of the Godhead, and He adored Him with profound submission as the Creator of His sacred humanity.

✤

Christ humbled Himself
in His Passion and death

"But He was not content with the humiliation of being a man: He emptied Himself still further, surrendering

[132] John 10:25.
[133] John 5:30.
[134] John 8:28.

completely His human will, and submitting even to the death of slaves, the ignominy of death by crucifixion."[135] As we contemplate the Crucified, we see the truth of the saying "The wood of the cross is the tree of knowledge."

Speaking of the Passion, St. Paul uses a phrase unique in itself and terrible to contemplate. He says that our blessed Lord was "made sin" for us.[136] Those words have come from the Holy Spirit. Long and reverently must we look at them, for in so doing we are peering into some of the most abysmal depths of Christ's sufferings. There, in His Passion and death, He reached the farthest limit of humility. The content of that singular phrase — "made sin" — shall never be exhausted by any finite intelligence.

"In Him dwelleth all the fullness of the Godhead corporeally,"[137] and because the plenitude of the Divinity was in our Lord, His sacred humanity shone with the beauty of God. To His soul and His body it imparted a divine loveliness. He was the perfect "image of the

---

[135] Boylan, *The Sunday Epistles and Gospels*, "Palm Sunday."
[136] 2 Cor. 5:21.
[137] Col. 2:9.

invisible God."[138] But when the dread hour of the Passion had at last loomed upon Him, He clothed Himself with our transgressions and was mantled in the degrading tatters of human depravity. Absolutely unresponsible, He assumed responsibility. Sinless, He became sin. A terrible paradox it was, the All-Holy and the All-Beautiful in such vile vesture. One has to remember His inconceivable abhorrence of sin, the repulsiveness with which He regarded it. But, ponder as we may, only our Lord Himself knows all the humiliation involved in His taking upon Himself the iniquities of mankind.

St. Thomas tells us that Christ suffered more than any individual man before or since. This in itself is a special consideration, but the extent and the nature of His sufferings are not now our immediate concern. We shall think not of the cruelty and pain and mental torture so much as of the *indignity* He underwent in all of them, finishing as they did in the supreme disgrace of the manner of His death. His Passion is one vast appalling humiliation. He underwent it freely and suffered with humble calmness. He humbled Himself even unto death; His earthly career went under in utter ignominy.

[138] Col. 1:15.

The Power of Humility

And all the time we have to remember *who* it is that was treated in such fashion, *who* it is that silently endured.

There was the moment when, standing before one of His judges, our Lord was asked about His followers and His doctrine. He requested the judge to interrogate the people who had heard Him, because He had given out His teaching quite publicly. Straightway, without any warning, He was struck on the face by an official. That sudden swift blow was a monstrous disrespect. It must have shot His head sideways painfully. It may even have excited quick laughter in the onlookers. And yet He received it with wonderful gentleness; humbly He remonstrated with the man who had so grossly insulted Him: "If I have spoken evil, show me what evil I have said, but if I have spoken well, why strike you me?"[139]

It would be very misleading to think that because our Lord was God, the endurance of pain and insult cost Him nothing; for this is to forget that, although He was divine, He was human as well, and like us in every way, with the solitary exception of sin.

Indeed, it is precisely on account of His Godhead that each act of scorn was all the more humiliating, all

[139] Cf. John 18:23.

the harder to bear. Most exalted was the majesty of Christ; ineffable His dignity. The excellences of His Godhead are infinitely beyond our small grasp.

What man, then, can measure the degradation of the scourging? What angel can fully estimate its indignity? The penalty of flogging is considered one of the lowest disgraces to which a man could be subjected. For an ordinary human being, it is infamous. Imagine the flagellation of Christ! See the violent activity of the soldiers. Listen to the rapid succession of sharp sounds, whips on flesh, the impact of lashes on the body of a Man-God. Notice the gradual change of the sounds: they become dull and sodden as the thongs become saturated with blood. . . .

And all through the dire thing, never did He murmur; never once was the calm of His mind ruffled. If you weigh all the circumstances, the insult to the Godhead, the savagery to His manhood, the utter shame, you realize what a marvelous example of humility it affords.

You see it again in what followed. The soldiers gathered the spiky branches of some shrub and (with care for their hands) plaited these thorny twigs, intertwining them in the rough, unsymmetrical shape of a crown. A crooked brambly diadem for a jeering coronation, it was pressed down upon Him and became tangled in His hair. Men made the Almighty seem ludicrous, with bits of a bush on His head, piercing Him sharply. And He received their sarcastic genuflections, their belittling of Him, while tiny trickles of blood came down His forehead from a hundred pinpoint stabbings, each with its separate sting.

It is difficult to bear ridicule and contempt, and more difficult when in pain. But the divine face was serene and bore the humiliation without shadow of annoyance — as also that other frightful act of contempt mentioned in the Gospel: "They did spit on Him."[140] This heinous disrespect was among the outrages singled apart beforehand in our Lord's mind, for He had told His Apostles it would occur.[141]

Even unto death He humbled Himself. So tremendous a mystery was that death that the sun veiled itself from the spectacle. During the three hours that He hung upon the Cross, "there was darkness over all the earth."[142] Crucifixion was a penalty introduced by the

---

[140] Mark 15:19.
[141] Luke 18:32.
[142] Luke 23:44.

Romans into Palestine; the Jews had never inflicted it on culprits. A retribution particularly for slaves found guilty of a grave misdemeanor, it is described as "the final and most terrible punishment of slaves."[143] To this ultimate infamy Christ, who had taken the form of a slave, was condemned.

On the same afternoon that the sentence was carried out, two men convicted of thieving were crucified with Him. He "was reputed with the wicked."[144] Vaguely in the dim light could the three tortured human shapes on the gibbets be seen. To think that the indistinct form on the middle Cross was the world's God. . . .

During the three long hours He hung from the nails, the cold breezes as of night blowing on His bare flesh, every nerve in Him was aquiver with agony. The sag of His body from His wounded hands was insufferable — and it was weighted in addition with the huge burden of our sins, for "the Lord hath laid on Him the iniquity of us all."[145] He could not rest it on His feet; they were pierced with a strong nail too. Not a move could He

[143] Cicero, *In Verr.*, 66.
[144] Isa. 53:12.
[145] Isa. 53:6.

make, not the slightest stir that would not aggravate His wounds and add to His sufferings. And if He just hung motionless, there was the slow dead-weight pull of the body downward.

Seven times His voice was heard, but never a word of protest. Once, it is true, He complained. Yet a complaint is different. It is only a cry of distress at experiencing great difficulty, although in the heart there is still submission. Such was that most mysterious of His utterances: "My God, my God, why hast Thou forsaken me?"[146] In a manner unknown to us, the dying Redeemer was abandoned by His Father. It is surmised that our Lord voluntarily permitted a dismal cloud to blot out the light and bliss of the Godhead from His human soul. He was accursed, solitary, His mind in nethermost depths of anguish, His body racked with torture; an outcast, "the most abject of men,"[147] bereft of His glory, His reputation gone.

Then at last the head sank on the breast. The paleness of death was on Him. He was very still. The divine tragedy was over.

[146] Matt. 27:46.
[147] Isa. 53:3.

Gaze at Him in such plight, and remember that the sacred humanity is the greatest and most exalted thing created in Heaven or on earth.

Humility means, as we have been told, a lowering of ourselves. Never can mankind witness a greater humility than this, for lower the sacred humanity of Christ could not descend. His Passion rebukes and confounds our pride.

༄

Christ humbles Himself in the Eucharist

For those who by grace can see with the eyes of faith, the humility of Christ goes on even yet. We have but to kneel before the tabernacle, and again we are confronted with it. The mystery of the Blessed Sacrament presents another and final form of our Lord's utter self-abasement. Both manhood and Godhead are lost to view. It is a double eclipse. In the tabernacle He is just as a thing a person puts away to keep; He has reduced Himself to the mode of an inanimate object.

Immediately before instituting the Blessed Eucharist, Christ performed an act of profound humility. He went on His knees before each of the Apostles in turn, bent down, and washed their feet. "Was it that in this moment He was seized, as it were, with a divine respect for these humble men . . . ? If He who is . . . the very Son of God so humbles Himself, what of us? It is one thing to humble oneself before a superior or an equal, but it is another thing to humble oneself before an inferior."[148]

Then into His sacred and venerable hands He took bread. There is nothing more common, the world over, than bread; nothing more ordinary. This is what He selected. Beneath its appearances He becomes present — a condescension beyond all thought of man or angel. So impressed was Cardinal Franzelin by the abjection of our Lord's state in the Blessed Sacrament, that, in his opinion, it explained how the Mass was a true sacrifice. The double consecration gives Christ an existence that is so lowly that it could be regarded as a sacrifice.

At any rate, the lowering of self, as already seen, is the essential act of humility. In this mystery, there is a reducing of self to a minimum that only our blessed Savior Himself in His love could have planned. Everything about this sacrament speaks of the virtue; the very name it bears tells us of it. *Eucharist* means "thanksgiving," and

[148] Fr. James, O.F.M. Cap., *The Spirit of Christ* (Westminster, Maryland: The Newman Bookshop, 1946), 129-130.

gratitude is always a humble thing, an acknowledgment of dependence and indebtedness.

Besides, who can fail to see humility in the helplessness to which our Lord, although Almighty, subjects Himself in the Eucharist?

He has to be borne from place to place; He does not shield Himself from insult. To be protected from profanation, He relies on others. Perfectly humble, He does nothing to defend Himself from sacrilege or to keep us from maltreating Him.

The virtue is again apparent in the smallness of the appearances beneath which He is present. The size is exiguous indeed, and yet the eternal marvel of the Faith is that underneath the diminutive species is contained Christ in all the richness of His divine Person, in the fullness of His two natures.

Christ's whole life in the Blessed Sacrament breathes humility. That life is hidden; very often it is lonely. Sometimes He meets with scant courtesy, and on occasions with disappointment and neglect. He is passed by without so much as a thought. Yet He remains, through the years, an abiding Presence. His humility is plain also in His constant availableness. Every day of the year He is easily found; any day we can approach Him. There is but one exception: the door of the tabernacle is open wide on Good Friday — the only day He is absent.

The Incarnation was an unspeakable condescension, a stooping down of the Lord from great heights to our lowliness. But as we adore the mystery of the Blessed Eucharist, it seems to us that here is an even greater abasement by far.

This is so especially when the mystery is considered under the aspect of Holy Communion. Jesus becomes the spiritual food of man. He Himself tells us that His flesh is truly the sustenance of our soul. "My flesh is meat indeed."[149] The mind should always hold in high relief the uttermost condescension of the Son of God in allowing us to take Him into our mortal bodies in the same manner that we take material things as food for our human life. It tells us strikingly of the deep, deep humility of the Savior of men.

⚘

Christ's example should move you to be humble

Such, in bare outline, is the virtue as it is seen in the crib, on the Cross, and in the tabernacle. When we

[149] John 6:56 (RSV = John 6:55).

reflect on the infinite greatness of God and then gaze at His lowliness in those three states, we are overwhelmed, but we can vaguely surmise how monstrous a pride is ours that has to be counteracted by such tremendous humility. The example of His virtue will always remain a cogent reason for us to follow, with the help of grace, in His footsteps.

Chapter Six

✣

How you can develop humility

We come now to review the means by which the virtue of humility may be attained.

At the outset, we must carefully note that recognizing we are proud is the beginning of humility. Moreover, no matter how much we practice the virtue, it would be false to believe we are humble, because the moment we think ourselves humble, we cease to be so in reality.[150]

The virtue is attainable; it must be, because God has commanded it. It is not for us, however, to know whether we have attained it. We should have a true desire for humility; and as long as we live, we must endeavor to acquire it, imploring God for it, being confident that

---

[150] Cf. Bergamo, *Humility of Heart*, 19.

He, the Lover of man's salvation, will not fail to give us so vital a grace.

Full emphasis has to be laid on the business of getting to know ourselves truly. To this, reference has already been made more than once. If humility may be regarded as the negative foundation of the virtues, self-knowledge is to be regarded as the very foundation of the foundation. It is the first thing, the initial work, in our interior life. Nobody properly begins otherwise. And it is a work that can never be laid aside, for God warned St. Catherine of Siena, "Beware that thou never leave the cell of self-knowledge."[151]

Always accompanying it is another science that is no less essential: the knowledge of God. Our Lord appeared one day to the saint and said, "Know, my daughter, what thou art and what I am. If thou canst learn these two things, thou art blessed indeed. I am He that is. Thou art that which is not. If thy soul is deeply penetrated with this truth, thou wilt never consent to transgress any one of my commandments, and easily wilt thou acquire grace, truth, and peace." The double knowledge required

---

[151] St. Catherine of Siena (1347-1380; Dominican tertiary), *Dialogue*, "A Treatise of Prayer."

is not a theoretical thing (which is easily won), but rather a practical consciousness, an intimate awareness: a live, deep conviction of our native nothingness, our personal sinfulness and the sublimity of God. This comes to us, through earnest prayer, from the Holy Spirit.

It is of advantage also to mingle lowly views of ourselves with our thoughts and prayers, just as we take bread with other kinds of food. Thus, when we kneel in the divine presence and consider the greatness of the Lord, we should at the same time reflect that we are nil; when we make an act of adoration, we should be mindful of our unworthiness; when we purpose to correct some fault, we should recall our past offenses and make an act of inward shame; when we ask God for some virtue, we should consider that of ourselves we are unable to attain it and that we do not deserve to receive it, while yet we maintain our trust in His infinite goodness; when we elicit sorrow for sin, we should reflect on our weakness. Such is the way, by continual exercise, to arrive at a deep and habitual knowledge of our own misery and to become rooted in this grace.[152]

[152] Cf. John Baptist Scaramelli, *Directorium Asceticum*, III, 421.

The Power of Humility

Humility, it is true, is necessary for salvation. It is not, of course, required that we possess the virtue in its fullness, but we must have a certain amount or degree of it. There is, therefore, a humility of *counsel* and a humility of *precept*. The latter consists in being subject to God to the extent of not offending Him gravely. It is obligatory on all Christians. All must be humble enough not to commit mortal sin. We are bound to have that reverential fear of the Lord which makes us mindful of what He has commanded — that fear and mindfulness which is said by St. Thomas to be the very root of the virtue.[153] But it would be most unwise to limit ourselves to this strictly necessary amount, for spiritual authorities warn us that those who confine themselves to what is absolutely essential will never really acquire the virtue.

A point must be made clear. At Baptism, God bestows on us the capability of performing acts of supernatural virtue. He infuses into our soul the power of exercising the humility that is necessary for us in order to believe and pray as we ought. This is infused humility. It is a permanent ability divinely imparted. It does not necessarily make the acts of the virtue easy, but it makes them

[153] *Summa Theologica*, II-II, Q. 161, art. 6.

possible. The facility is won by practice; ease comes from making use of the God-granted power. If we exercise the humility we have received, the virtue is strengthened and increased. From practice we gradually get the acquired humility of which St. Thomas speaks, which is the infused virtue developed by God's grace and our human diligence.

ৎ

Pray

Among the means of attaining humility, the chief place must be given to prayer. It is a sure method. In vain shall we try to be humble; to little purpose shall we study the virtue or reflect upon the reasons for its practice. All goes for naught unless we sincerely and frequently beseech God and His Blessed Mother to grant it, relying on His promise that if we ask, we certainly shall receive all things needful for our salvation.

To pray *sincerely* for humility presupposes that we want it. Obviously, we shall never be humble unless we really desire to be. And we cannot desire humility if we have not learned to love it; nor can we love it until we come to realize that it is a precious thing, essential to our eternal welfare, and that it is in a sense "the greatest good."

The following prayers will be found useful:

❧

Litany of Humility

Lord, have mercy on us.
Christ, have mercy on us.
Lord, have mercy on us.

Jesus, meek and humble of Heart,
hear us.

Jesus, meek and humble of Heart,
graciously hear us.

From the desire of being esteemed,
deliver me, O Jesus.

From the desire of being loved,
deliver me, O Jesus.

From the desire of being sought after,
deliver me, O Jesus.

From the desire of being praised,
deliver me, O Jesus.

From the desire of being honored,
deliver me, O Jesus.

From the desire of being preferred,
deliver me, O Jesus.

From the desire of being consulted,
deliver me, O Jesus.

From the desire of being approved,
deliver me, O Jesus.

From the desire of being spared,
deliver me, O Jesus.

From the fear of being humbled,
deliver me, O Jesus.

From the fear of being despised,
deliver me, O Jesus.

From the fear of being rebuked,
deliver me, O Jesus.

From the fear of being calumniated,
deliver me, O Jesus.

From the fear of being forgotten,
deliver me, O Jesus.

From the fear of being laughed at,
deliver me, O Jesus.

From the fear of being made game of,
deliver me, O Jesus.

From the fear of being insulted,
deliver me, O Jesus.

O Mary, Mother of the humble,
pray for me.

St. Joseph, protector of humble souls,
pray for me.

St. Michael, who wert the first
to trample upon pride,
pray for me.

All the just, sanctified by humility,
pray for me.

O Jesus, whose first lesson has been
"Learn of me, for I am meek
and humble of Heart,"
*teach me to become humble of
heart like Thee.*[154]

[154] Thibault, *Abbot Columba Marmion*, 53.

*

Lord, I do not even know
what humility is like,
but I know that I do not possess it
and cannot of myself obtain it,
and that unless I have it,
I shall not be saved.

Therefore it only remains
for me to ask it of Thee.
But give me the grace to ask it as I ought.
Thou hast promised, O my God,
to grant me all those things
which I shall ask of Thee
and which are necessary
for my eternal salvation.
And humility being most necessary
for me, faith compels me to believe
that Thou wilt grant me this,
if I know how to ask it of Thee.

But herein lies the difficulty,
because I know not how to
ask Thee as I ought.

Teach me and help me, that I may pray to Thee
as Thou dost wish me to pray and in that
efficacious manner in which Thou Thyself
knowest that I shall be heard.

And as Thou commandest me
to be humble, I am ready to obey.
But grant that through Thy help I may
in truth become such as Thou dost desire.

I ardently desire to be humble;
and whence comes this love and
desire for humility, if not from Thee,
who hast put it into my heart by Thy holy grace?
Oh, of Thy goodness grant me therefore
what Thou hast made me to love and desire.
I hope for it, and I will continue to hope for it.

"Strengthen me, O Lord God, that,
as Thou hast promised, I may bring to pass
that which I have purposed,
having a belief that it
might be done by Thee."[155]

[155] Jth. 13:7. This prayer is taken from Bergamo's *Humility of Heart*, 18.

How you can develop humility

Contemplate God's greatness

The masters of the spiritual life tell us that prayerful pondering on the divine attributes leads us to the virtue of humility. It is by comparison that things are effectively known. A poor man, for instance, will never have a true idea of his poverty until he sees the palatial residences and halls and apartments of the rich. So, too, we may know after a fashion that we are nothing, but we will not have a true knowledge of self nor be humble until we contrast ourselves with the infinite perfections of the Lord. Then it is that the supereminence of the Almighty shows us our nothingness. By contemplating His greatness, we discover our lowliness, and by gazing on His purity, we see how soiled we are interiorly. Such a consideration of the Deity fosters deep reverence in our heart, and of that reverence virtue is born.

We speak of the perfections of God. It is more accurate to say that He is one simple, absolute perfection. God does not share our virtues; rather He is a single infinite virtue. His power, wisdom, goodness, and other attributes are divided and distinguished only by our mind, but in reality they are all one, for His attributes make no multiplicity in the Eternal Being.

The Power of Humility

Whatever good is found in creatures, God has it to an unlimited degree. Statements made of God fall infinitely short of Him; ideas formed of Him fail to approach Him. St. Augustine says that He unspeakably transcends every likeness of Himself in any creature. Beyond all thought, God surpasses immeasurably the range of even angelic intellect. God is the Tremendous Mystery.

But it cannot be denied that by means of creatures, we acquire some knowledge of Him. When we think of the creation of the world, we are struck with the divine omnipotence: for creation presupposes infinite power. Scientists say the number of stars in the universe probably equals the number of grains of sand on the seashores of this world. The majority of them are hundreds of thousands of times greater than our earth; some are millions and millions of times greater. All these the Almighty has poised in space unfathomable. And He has peopled the heavens with a vast concourse of beings, an angelic host that theologians consider is more numerous than the human race.

Were we to travel to the outside of all things, we would find God far off still, as incomprehensible to our mind as ever, for His immensity is such that "the heaven of heavens cannot contain Him."[156] And if stars and angels and men and earth were to wither away and be entirely effaced in their own original nothingness, the grandeur of God would in no wise be impaired; upon the splendor of His majesty there would not be the slightest trace of the vanished creation. He dwells in the supreme solitude of unapproachable light. Thoughts like these should occasionally be brought to mind as we kneel before the tabernacle.

Creatures pass on and away. From all eternity God has been God. He purely is — unalterable, without past or future, the changeless "Spectator of the centuries." With difficulty our mind grasps a little knowledge, and in the process there is much liability to error. Not so with God. He sees all that actually is, all that is possible, all that has been or will be. "Oh, the depths of the riches of the wisdom and knowledge of God," exclaims St. Paul.[157]

God being infinitely good and infinitely holy, all created goodness and all created holiness are but the palest and remotest reflection of His sanctity.

[156] Cf. 3 Kings 8:27 (RSV = 1 Kings 8:27).
[157] Rom. 11:33.

The Power of Humility

From such reflections we arrive at a profound esteem for the Lord Almighty, the Immense Monarch and Ultimate End of the whole world. We should sincerely confess that He is the Infinite All for whom it is impossible not to be, who is not liable to imperfection or change, who is infinitely happy and blessed in the possession of Himself, deriving no addition from any creature; that He is that Being who communicates being to all things, that Power who gives us our powers, that Immense Holiness from whom comes all human and angelic holiness, that Inexhaustible Fountain of grace who imparts grace to men, that Uncreated Perfection who alone can make creatures perfect, that Unlimited Glory who alone can fully satisfy the soul that loves and serves Him.

When we meditate thus on the ineffable Godhead, we see more vividly that we have as our own merely nonbeing by nature, plus our sins. We bow down in a keener consciousness that He is all and that we are nothing.

༈

Meditate on Christ's Passion

The Passion of our divine Lord has already been treated as a *reason* for cultivating the virtue of humility. It is also a *method*, much recommended for its efficacy. If we contemplate the Son of God, who is majesty itself, so deeply abased on Calvary, so humble before His Father under the shameful vesture of our sins, so submissive even to the executioners — if we direct our eyes to the divine sufferings, we shall be rescued by Christ from the snare of pride.[158] Frequent reflection on the Passion leads us far, for there is a wonderful power in it, an influence that moves out upon the soul.

↝

Imitate Mary

And now let us come in spirit into the gentle presence of her who has been styled the Magnificence of God. We are reminded by St. Grignion de Montfort that true devotion to Our Lady inspires the soul to imitate particularly her profound humility.[159] Hers was the most faithful reproduction ever made of the total self-abasement of her Son. St. Bonaventure assigns, as one reason for her enthronement as Queen of Heaven, the

[158] Cf. Ps. 24:15 (RSV = Ps. 25:15).

[159] St. Louis Grignion de Montfort (1673-1716; secular priest who founded the Sisters of the Divine Wisdom and the Missionary Priests of Mary), *True Devotion to Mary*.

fact that she possessed this virtue more eminently than any other being.[160] "She esteemed herself," he says, "as nothing whatsoever." Had we only the angel's testimony that she was "full of grace,"[161] we would be warranted in concluding that she was most humble. Where there is grace, there also is humility. Where there is the fullness of grace, there is the perfection of humility. If we knew only that she was the Mother of God, we could safely infer — because of her intimate nearness to the Incarnate Almighty — that she was singularly and surpassingly humble.

As soon as her most holy name adorns St. Luke's Gospel, and the angel comes with the light of Heaven around him, the lowliness of her heart is immediately seen. When she consented to the divine plan of the Incarnation and was forthwith exalted to a dignity in some sort infinite, she confessed that she was only the *slave* of God. This is what our Lady meant when she used the word "handmaid."[162] See, on the one hand, the excellence of her rank as Mother of God, a peerless

[160] *Sermo* 3, *de Assumpt.*, *B.M.V.*

[161] Luke 1:28.

[162] Luke 1:38.

privilege that places her next to the Almighty Himself; and on the other hand, see her deeming herself to be in the lowest human condition known. It is a perfect example of the self-abjection proper to humility.

Elizabeth, greeting her as blessed among women, is mindful of the exquisite condescension of Mary's visit and wonders how she could have deserved to have the Mother of her Lord come to her. Mary was conscious of her own exceptional graces; but if every generation of men would acclaim her blessed, she acknowledged that it was because He who is mighty had wrought "great things" in her,[163] that from Him had come the wonder of divine Motherhood and the other supernatural marvels consequent upon it. As the humble always do, she referred all back to God.

We could quote many other instances of that lowliness which so pleased the Lord. Suffice it to say that Mary's Immaculate Heart is an abyss of humility. But since it is also a throne of mercy before which all her children may confidently kneel, we may be sure that if we pray and try to copy her dispositions, however remotely, she will not fail us.

[163] Luke 1:49.

The Power of Humility

✻

Perform acts of humility

These are so many methods of acquiring humility. We will now consider one final means, indispensable and more surely effective than even the most devout prayer.

We have it on the authority of St. Bernard that we cannot be humble unless we are humbled, and that humiliation is the way to humility, just as study leads to knowledge.

Humiliation is of two kinds: we can be humbled by ourselves and by others.

Reference has already been made to acts of the virtue performed of our own accord to foster it. Further instances of such acts would be deference to the opinions of others; restricted use of the pronoun *I*; disesteem for our own judgments; keeping ourselves in the background; various courtesies shown both to those over us and to those inferior to us; and avoidance of criticism (which is always a sign of pride).

It is an act of humility to remain untroubled when no consolation is granted during prayer — provided we realize that we are not being cheated if we, who are nothing and deserve nothing, are given nothing.

How you can develop humility

It is good also to consider our evil tendencies and the many failures from which God has done everything to deliver us. Faults, no matter how great, become the occasion of much spiritual advantage when they make us realize our misery and powerlessness, when they make us see that without grace we can accomplish nothing, and bring us to a firm reliance on God, in whom we can do all things. It is possible indeed to humble ourselves secretly at every moment before God and before our fellowman.

Knowing the Lord's majesty, we can humble ourselves for fearing Him so little; knowing His goodness, we can humble ourselves for loving Him so poorly. If we see an erring brother, we can exercise humility by reflecting that we could suddenly become worse; if we notice some supernatural gift in him, we can consider that he corresponds with grace better than we.

Rendering thanks to God for the benefits we have received is an excellent act of humility, because thanksgiving teaches us to acknowledge the divine Giver. "In all things give thanks: for this is the will of God in Christ concerning you all."[164]

[164] 1 Thess. 5:18.

The Power of Humility

ж

Accept humiliations from others

These various self-humiliations should be practiced. But it is well to bear in mind that in acts of humility freely undertaken, we are exposed to the danger of vainglory. There lurks in self-love a craftiness and a guile that make us try to win esteem even while appearing to seek contempt. This is that spurious humility the masters warn us against. It is, of course, hypocrisy.

No such danger is present in humiliations caused us by others. They are brought about by life's vicissitudes independent of our will. They come unexpectedly. Rightly can we regard them as God's choosing.

He may allow us to fail in some undertaking; it is a humiliation directly sent by Him to cure our pride. Or He may send us humiliations indirectly through our fellow creatures. These humblings are never what we would personally choose, but they are sent to us by the will of God. He knows our weak point, and with sureness these sudden humiliations are aimed at it. All God's love is in the aim, for He wishes to heal our pride. Someone in authority will admonish; he will overlook us in giving offices or in bestowing attention and sympathy. Colleagues will treat us awkwardly; they will contradict or pass disparaging remarks about our work; they will show a lack of due regard; they will ask another for his opinion, as if ours were of little use; they will show anger at an inoffensive word.

All these slights and many more may originate from inadvertence or from frailty or (very rarely) from malice. But it should not matter. Those who humble us do us a genuine service. If we are right-minded, we shall look upon them as instruments God has chosen to cure our spiritual wounds. We shall not censure their conduct, but rather reprove our own sensitiveness, which is so quick to take offense, and our pride, which refuses to be crushed.

Our acceptance of these involuntary humiliations is a sign of true and sincere humility. Borne patiently, they have upon us a sanctifying power. The infallible proof of humility is patience, but only when it proceeds from the recognition of our personal unworthiness and when we endure the wrong because we know we have received our deserts.

Few, however, use such afflictions as a means of acquiring the virtue. "They are," as St. Bernard says, "humbled without being made humble." We are advised against comforting ourselves in trials by thinking that they will soon end, or that they are mere formalities to be gone through before we become more favorably circumstanced. We shall always need humiliations. They are required for expiation, for progress, and for perseverance. They are required as long as any trace of pride remains to be removed.

St. Thomas assures us that "acquired humility is, in a way, the greatest good,"[165] and the truth of this statement cannot escape anyone who considers the reasons for the virtue and our Lord's teaching about its necessity for salvation. Yet, strangely enough, according to spiritual writers, humility is what we neglect most of all. This little book should not be laid aside without our resolving to begin work — a resolution of urgent importance.

[165] *De verit.*, I, I.

Fr. Canice Bourke, O.F.M. Cap.

Fr. Canice Bourke, O.F.M. Cap.
(1890-1969)

No stranger to the virtue of humility, Fr. Canice was keenly aware of the gifts God had given him and spent his life using those gifts to serve God and His people.

Born Edward Bourke in Kilkenny, Ireland, he joined the Capuchin Order in his late teens and took the religious name of Canice, the patron of his native city. He studied at the Capuchin College in Rochestown, County Cork, and earned a bachelor's degree at University College Cork.

Fr. Canice spent his priesthood giving missions and retreats and became known throughout Ireland for his effective, energetic preaching. For many years, he served as Commissary Provincial of the Third Order of St.

Francis and was twice elected Definitor of the Irish Province.

In addition to his writings on the Faith, which include a standard work on the Blessed Mother, Fr. Canice authored many delightful essays in the Irish language and some unusual short stories in English.

As with his dynamic preaching, Fr. Canice continues, through his writings, to lead today's Christians to a profound realization of the nature of man and the majesty and awesome gifts of God.

✣

Sophia Institute Press®

Sophia Institute™ is a nonprofit institution that seeks to restore man's knowledge of eternal truth, including man's knowledge of his own nature, his relation to other persons, and his relation to God. Sophia Institute Press® serves this end in numerous ways: it publishes translations of foreign works to make them accessible to English-speaking readers; it brings out-of-print books back into print; and it publishes important new books that fulfill the ideals of Sophia Institute™. These books afford readers a rich source of the enduring wisdom of mankind.

Sophia Institute Press® makes these high-quality books available to the general public by using advanced technology and by soliciting donations to subsidize its general publishing costs. Your generosity can help Sophia

Institute Press® to provide the public with editions of works containing the enduring wisdom of the ages. Please send your tax-deductible contribution to the address below. We also welcome your questions, comments, and suggestions.

For your free catalog, call:
Toll-free: 1-800-888-9344

or write:
Sophia Institute Press®
Box 5284, Manchester, NH 03108

or visit our website:
www.sophiainstitute.com

Sophia Institute™ is a tax-exempt institution
as defined by the Internal Revenue Code,
Section 501(c)(3). Tax I.D. 22-2548708.